Awakening
as Holy Mystery

"This book will delight many as the author explores a renewed understanding and language for a deeper intimacy with God and maturity of the soul rooted in Christ. Although language is always limited in its ability to express the ineffable, the author identifies resonances in the wisdom of other traditions and offers expansive expressions in Christian liturgies and prayers. He immerses the reader in our unity with Christ through the language of belovedness. Those seeking that intimacy with God will be drawn into the reflections, prayers, and liturgy, all suffused with belovedness in God. This is profoundly needed in an age of deep uncertainties and anxiety."

—**LINDA NICHOLLS**, Retired Primate, Anglican Church of Canada

"Through deep contemplative reflections, as well as resources for personal prayer and communal worship, Thew Forrester invites us on a journey beyond dualistic God-language into the possibility of awakening to and as Holy Mystery—a blossoming of our own Christ heart in lives of devotion and service. This book is a gift to the Christian community and to all who desire to know the potential of their own humanness."

—**MATTHEW WRIGHT**, Episcopal Priest

"Kevin Thew Forrester's exploration of Holy Mystery is a rich, multi-dimensional tapestry of imagery, metaphor, and spiritual wisdom. It is a set of resources full of surprises; the language is playful, exuberant, and earnest. I'm especially grateful that he included evocative open questions alongside the set of reflections; many of these have served me in my journal writing and for deeper awakening to the teachings. I also value the thoughtful language and inclusive invitation in all the creative liturgies for worship. Perhaps what moves me the most in his book are the meaningful prayers offered as resources for faith communities or for solitude practice. Here is a passionate and timely wake up call to entering a mature spiritual life, and I hope this book finds itself in the hands of many. I am glad I am one of them."

—**DAN HINES**, Retreat Leader, Coach, Poet, Priest, Sailor

Awakening as Holy Mystery

Realizing Christ Heart

Kevin G. Thew Forrester
Foreword by Richard F. Groves

WIPF & STOCK · Eugene, Oregon

AWAKENING AS HOLY MYSTERY
Realizing Christ Heart

Copyright © 2025 Kevin G. Thew Forrester. All rights reserved. Except for brief quotations in critical publications or reviews, no part of this book may be reproduced in any manner without prior written permission from the publisher. Write: Permissions, Wipf and Stock Publishers, 199 W. 8th Ave., Suite 3, Eugene, OR 97401.

Wipf & Stock
An Imprint of Wipf and Stock Publishers
199 W. 8th Ave., Suite 3
Eugene, OR 97401

www.wipfandstock.com

PAPERBACK ISBN: 979-8-3852-4653-3
HARDCOVER ISBN: 979-8-3852-4654-0
EBOOK ISBN: 979-8-3852-4655-7

VERSION NUMBER 07/16/25

Scripture quotations are from New Revised Standard Version Bible, copyright © 1989 National Council of the Churches of Christ in the United States of America. Used by permission. All rights reserved worldwide.

Scripture quotations marked *NNT* are from *A New New Testament: A Bible for the Twenty-First Century, Combining Traditional and Newly Discovered Texts*, ed. Hal Taussig (New York: Houghton Mifflin Harcourt, 2013).

Dedicated to the precious teachers
who graciously received and guided
this soul
on the path of awakening to
longing and love
for the Beloved—
the I of my i.

In all my senses; in heart, intellect, and conscience;
when I am drunk and bewildered with the desire of love;
and in the pain of the moments when I am separated from my beloved;
in my uncertain soul that burns with longing—it is You, only You!

HILMI, AWAKENED DREAMS

It is this interior sense of actually existing in this moment
as a sheer "I am" that is the real living person.

BRUTEAU, *RADICAL OPTIMISM*

I am as certain as I am that I am a [human being]
that nothing is so "near" to me as God.
God is nearer to me than myself.

ECKHART, "SERMON NINE"

You are the center without any edge.
You are I am, and I am, too.
I am your being.
My soul lives as You.

KEVIN G. THEW FORRESTER, P. 77

The Father and I are One.

JOHN 10:30 *NNT*

Contents

Author's Note | ix
Foreword by Richard F. Groves | xi
Acknowledgments | xiii
Introduction | xv

Part One: Awakening
  Reflection 1: Christ Heart: Awakening as Holy Mystery | 3
  Reflection 2: Christianity as a Nondual Spiritual Path | 17
  Reflection 3: Meditation Through the Wisdom of Eckhart | 23

Part Two: Unfolding
  Reflection 4: Celebrating the Curious Christ Soul | 41
  Reflection 5: Dawning of Christ Consciousness | 45
  Reflection 6: Becoming the Fullness of What We Already Are | 51
  Reflection 7: Living Christs of Touch | 58
  Reflection 8: The Courage to See | 64
  Reflection 9: Holy Wisdom | 70
  Reflection 10: Fishing to Friending | 79
  Reflection 11: Holy Mystery's Presence | 84

Part Three: Worship as Support
  Reflection 12: Liturgy: Support for Awakening | 93
  Reflection 13: Born and Reborn Again | 106
  Reflection 14: Grateful and Communal Creatures | 147

CODA: Participating in the Song of Life | 153

PART FOUR: PRAYERS & PSALMS TO NURTURE | 157

Bibliography | 229

Author's Note

QUOTATIONS FROM THE CANONICAL Scriptures are from the New Revised Standard Version (NRSV) unless otherwise noted. Extracanonical quotations are drawn from various sources, which are noted as such in the text. Whether the source be canonical or extracanonical, they resonate with this heart as sacred and wise.

Foreword

AWAKENING AS HOLY MYSTERY is a fresh, insightful, and masterful map for describing the soul's journey. The author blends his vast, extraordinary scholarship with pastoral clarity to produce a unique manual for today's spiritual seeker. This book is an important contribution regarding the stages of faith development, offering a deeper glimpse into the mystery of how we come to experience belief beyond the confines of narrow religious categories. Seekers will also gain new insights into the meaning of nondual Christianity through abundant insights from the world's great mystical traditions. Everything in this book invites us toward Christ-Heart-Consciousness and its radical vision for ourselves and the world.

Awakening as Holy Mystery is profoundly integral—weaving lessons from psychology, philosophy, history, and parallels from both Eastern and Western spiritual traditions. In addition to being a rich compendium, the author creatively intersperses courageous questions for personal reflection and exploration. As we are reminded that the soul's journey leads from the head to the heart, each chapter is like a living school for the soul where the Beloved comes to us, not separate from life but disguised in the events of everyday life. Among the quotes from countless great teachers, the reader is continually drawn back to the self-reflective nature of the spiritual journey where we are born again and over and over again . . . until, as in the Gospel of Thomas, "when you finally come to know yourselves, you will be known" (1:3).

Awakening as Holy Mystery is also a practical source of fresh, prayerful expressions and creative liturgical possibilities. Persons who engage in formal or informal ministries will be inspired by the variety of new formulas offered in the final chapters for both personal and group prayer. Ultimately, this work is a rare anthology produced by someone whose work

Foreword

of a lifetime has produced a classic integration of theology and practice in an utterly grounded, holistic way. It is one of those rare books that will be returned to over a lifetime as the soul journeys toward the Beloved.

Richard Groves, Founder
Sacred Art of Living Center, Bend, Oregon
April 21, 2025

Acknowledgments

FRIENDS ARE STEADFAST COMPANIONS of the heart and essential to the spiritual path. Jesus acknowledged this when his soul spoke forth, "I have called you friends" (John 15:15). I travel this path of awakening with friends whose wisdom guides, confronts, consoles, encourages, and shares the deepest darkness and the brightest joy. They embody and reveal Holy Mystery, and their presence is that rare gift for which my only response is grateful love. Without you, I am not. Sarah. Kip. Sheryl. Ziad. Julane. Joan. Katherine. Stephen. Diane.

Introduction

DRIVING AT EARLY DUSK through the giant redwoods north of San Francisco, my girlfriend (later, wife) and I were invited by the silent song of these ancient souls to stop, behold, touch, and listen. Their mysterious beauty drew me to lay my outstretched arms upon the mossy skin of one of these holy witnesses. We stood enveloped in the womb of the azure heavens and the moist earth, soul to soul, as the silent song bid me to awaken in that moment to the Deep arising as a simple and giant tree.

Awakening as Holy Mystery is simple, direct, and always in the present moment, whatever that moment might be. The moment is a womb, pulsating with a primordial strength capable of birthing our soul from sleep into life, if we but hear and respond with a sincere heart.

This book is a compilation of reflections and explorations on awakening. To hold it with an open soul and to engage its contents with sincerity is to become a participant in the spiritual practice of faith exploration. Faith exploration is one of the primary spiritual practices of awakening as Holy Mystery, an investigation into the spiritual meaning of the moment we are in. Faith means trusting in the presence of Holy Mystery as the given moment and our experience of that moment: a touch, a tear, a laugh, a loss, a sorrow. Faith involves discovering how to relax, receive, and follow the stream of life present in the moment. Faith is not to be confused with belief or doctrine. Faith is rooted in the immersion of our experience of the moment, a moment pregnant with the presence of Holy Mystery that transforms our consciousness, inviting surrender and devotion.

Three other essential supports integral to our soul's awakening are meditation, worship (devotion through liturgy), and breath/body/movement. My reflections here will not delve into breath/body/movement but

Introduction

will focus on the practices of meditation and worship (individual as well as communal) as part of the rich fabric of Reality that is our life.

I invite you to receive these reflections and explorations as invitations to develop your own spiritual practice of becoming a reflective soul. The Silence from which every creature emerges as a holy word sung into being always speaks to us, like the redwood reaching into my heart during an evening drive. There is no moment that is not replete with the Mystery of love. The Beloved awaits only the turn of our head to be seen (Julian of Norwich).[1] The gate of our heart must open to receive the Guest who never leaves (Rumi).[2]

I will introduce you to Holy Mystery—as Beloved, as Spirit, as Reality, as Source, as Ground, and more. The truth is that the love of which we speak is boundless (which is why it is Holy). The more our heart discovers, the more we want to know (with our heart and our body) about this Beloved, mysterious in its infinite capacity to be known, never shy to be questioned. Here we are receiving and being received by a Beloved with a boundless openness for intimacy. Loving is a knowing that never ends and never tires; but it does resolve, or dissolve into empty silence that is Spirit, which makes Reality a Mystery. Together we shall explore Holy Mystery.

Awakening as Holy Mystery is the birthing of Christ heart. Jesus fell in love with Holy Mystery, whom he experienced as his tender and tenacious Abba. Maturing in this loving relationship is how he came to realize his Christ heart. He invites us, as followers of the Christic path, to the same realization. We come to know Holy Mystery and ourself through the path of maturing love. From the silence of the womb, he emerges as one whose very life speaks of love, and so he is known as the Word of God (the voice of Holy Mystery). We are invited to that same spiritual path as we follow the deepest longing of our heart. From within the infinite Deep that is our origin a voice calls to us, often faint, but distant only for our part—because the Deep is the Source from which our life flows every moment.

In parts 1 and 2, "Awakening" and "Unfolding," we will discover that Holy Mystery is not an object, but the Love of our life, the Love that is our life. Jewish philosopher Martin Buber hints at the depths of this relationship when he speaks of the I-Thou relationship.[3] Holy Mystery is the Thou

---

1. Julian, *Showings*, 267.
2. Rumi, *Essential Rumi*, 109.
3. Buber, *I and Thou*.

Introduction

of our love. But even closer than a Thou, because the Thou remains a distanced object, or an *other*, of vision and speech.[4]

In part 3, "Worship as Support," I offer liturgical prayers—both individual and communal—to encourage, sustain, and guide our falling in love, our surrender, and our devotion to the Beloved. On the whole, I am aware of the difficulties with the word *worship*, as it tends to connote a magical or mythical divinity who stands as an object over and against us. But that need not be the case. In the end, as in the beginning, in worship we behold Holy Mystery because we are beheld. We see with the eyes of boundless love. Distinction without any division is one of the mysteries of love, through and through.[5]

In parts 1 through 3, "Awakening," "Unfolding," and "Worship as Support," each reflection is followed by the chance to inquire for yourself—and hopefully in partnership with another—where you are in the present moment. (However, "Reflection 13: Born and Reborn Again" also offers substantive liturgical resources for individual and communal use.) I encourage you to find a partner or two with whom to read and experience these reflections. Awakening, although exquisitely personal, is not solitary, because we are interdependent. We are conceived and gestate within the being of our mother. Every feeling, each thought, all our body sensations arise in the womb of relationship. In our personal existence we arise also as social beings within given worlds of languages, arts, and cultures. We are attached, for good and for ill, to other beings. Our healing, constitutive of our awakening, unfolds in and through our attachments, specifically with our significant others. Awakening is not simply the fruition of meditation and personal inquiry, but a birthing of new life requiring the shedding of misconceptions, prejudices, ignorance, etc., much of which happens through conversation that enables us to transcend the limitations of our current perspective for one more inclusive.[6]

The reflections offer the chance to be curious and explore. In a dyad or triad in which we experience security and safety, our body can relax and our heart open enabling our soul to explore and even soar.[7] This beloved field of exploration is an invitation for sincere wonderment about what is

---

4. Beatrice Bruteau speaks of this nondual union as an I-I relationship, which is a lovely and apt description. Bruteau, *Radical Optimism*, 111–12.

5. See Wilber, *Integral Spirituality*, 159–61.

6. See Wilber, *Integral Spirituality*, 142–62.

7. An excellent resource is Dana, *Polyvagal Theory in Therapy*.

Introduction

truly happening in heart, body, and mind—the three centers of the soul. I invite you to receive each reflection as an invitation for intimacy from your spiritual lover that is Holy Mystery. The only desire of your Beloved is to be known and loved, which is to know your own soul, through and through, as love.

Part 4, "Prayers & Psalms to Nurture," includes a prayer upon awakening (or Matins), a simple body-based movement prayer ("Abwun Gesture of Oneness"), a morning liturgy ("Abiding Liturgy for Morning"), as well as soulful reflections for each week of the year. Prayer is the heart's conversation with its true love. Here are the soul's musings, cries, bewilderments, longings, wonderments, songs, pleas, and so much more. These prayers and psalms collect the focus of our soul and invite us to sit with, explore, cry with, and feel gratitude for the gift of boundless love that is Holy Mystery. They do not offer answers. They express the soul's longing to know the kiss of grace in every nook and cranny of her daily life. You might find it helpful to frame your reading, conversation, and inquiries of parts 1 and 2, with the weekly prayers and psalms of part 4. The key to spiritual practice is to root your reading in your present experience, so that the knowledge you realize arises from and is validated by your personal experience.

PART ONE

Awakening

Reflection 1

Christ Heart
Awakening as Holy Mystery

> The ruined hearts are God's stores of treasure;
> great treasures are buried in these ruins.
>
> "The True Kaaba," in *Love's Ripening: Rumi on the Heart's Journey*

WHAT IS A HEART alive with compassion and joy and spontaneity? A heart not continually weighed down by drivenness, anger, and fear? A heart at rest? A heart wholly embodied, not walled off in pain and searching for someone or something to hurt?

This is Christ heart, which is a heart awakened as Holy Mystery.[1] This is a human being—a self—who is aware and alive and engaged with the world in its suffering and its longing to be free.

Our awakening as Holy Mystery is our maturation as a human being. We don't mature in a vacuum. Our sense of self, which includes our relationships with others and the wider environment, and which will mature over the decades, is inchoately present from our earliest postpartum moments,

---

1. I was first introduced to the language of Holy Mystery while working on my initial master's degree reading Karl Rahner's *Foundations of Christian Faith*. His theology has remained foundational and seminal since.

and perhaps in the womb. Our earliest self is like a porous grain of sand with the inherent potential to be a precious pearl birthed in and through the experiences of life shaped through the crucible of our relationships.

LOOKING AND LONGING

It is amazing that from birth we have an emerging sense of self.

> Between two and six months, infants consolidate their sense of a core self as a separate, cohesive, bounded, physical unit, with a sense of their own agency, affectivity, and continuity in time. . . . Our subjective experiences of union with another can occur only after a sense of a core self and a core other exists. Union experiences are thus viewed as the successful result of actively organizing the experience of self-being-with-another. The period of life from roughly nine to eighteen months is not primarily devoted to the developmental tasks of independence or autonomy or individuation—that is, of getting away and free from the primary caregiver. It is equally devoted to the seeking and creating of *intersubjective union with another*.[2]

During the earliest months of life (as well as throughout our life) we are learning new forms of self-being-with-another. The sense of who we are—that is, our sense of self—is a gradual integration of the many relationships and their felt impact on our being. We have an ever-evolving sense of our self (separate and cohesive) in ever-changing relationships with other selves (also separate and cohesive) and there is the affective bond, or felt feeling, between the two. This psychological dynamic is known as an object relation. The felt feeling we long for most—and it is more than a feeling—is that of fullness, rest, completion: qualities of love. In the language of spiritual poetry, our young heart, in and through our many relationships, is searching for the Holy Land, the New Jerusalem, the garden of Eden, of the soul.

There are many names in poetry, all signifying that the deepest longing of the human heart is universal. We are longing for that *something* that will bring us rest, allow us a secure inner peace, and set us free from being driven by so many things. This, at least, is how the spiritual journey often initially is experienced and understood. We are searching for that *object* that will fully and completely satisfy the soul.

---

2. Stern, *Interpersonal World*, 10; emphasis added.

We long to sense in our bones that we are whole, complete, beautiful—perfect as we are with all our imperfections. We are seeking love; love that abides without fail, and that invites our soul into wondrous exploration of this present moment, and all such moments, whatever they might be. This is true freedom. The capacity to be the truth of what we are regardless of circumstance. This is love without conditions. Boundless love.

I find it helpful to distinguish three stages in the human spiritual journey: discovery of Holy Mystery, living with Holy Mystery, and awakening as Holy Mystery. The spiritual journey is the unfolding path of becoming an authentic, free, spontaneous, and thriving human being. (Sometimes this is characterized as a self that is fully alive.) The fruit of this journey, in our awakening as Holy Mystery, is also the realization of being Christ heart. We awaken as a compassionate, joyful, person aware that all creatures are innately good because their true nature is Holy Mystery.

DISCOVERY OF HOLY MYSTERY

For most of us there are early experiences of love touching our soul. Maybe it's when a neighbor gazed gently into your eyes as they lifted you from the pavement after having fallen and skinned your knees badly. As their eyes met yours there was simple kindness, generosity without measure. Although you couldn't name it at the time, you felt safe in a pool of boundless love in their kind and gentle eyes. Or perhaps a friend or parent embraced your shoulder as you slumped under the weight of having failed to be accepted into a group or club or team. Or there was a time you laid upon the soft July grass, grounded upon Mother Earth, relaxing as the endless azure sky bathed your being. We each have our experiences.

Each of these is an initial experience of boundless love that unfolds without end. Love is not a thing but the texture of life itself—its spiritual fabric. Life-as-love is graciously enfolding our self and inviting us to trustingly unfold. We have an inchoate sense that we are whole, we are complete, and we are beautiful. This incipient feeling of innate goodness then rubs up against our daily experiences of being not enough, inadequate, incomplete, and dissatisfied. Love as our spiritual fabric tends to recede into the chimeric realm of faded memory.

Our soul has been partially awakened, however, in these powerful experiences of grace. They remind us, not consciously[3] for the most part, that

---

3. Daniel Stern, from the discipline of psychotherapy, provides clarification of the

we arise from a Source that is good, and as that arising, we are primordially whole—regardless of what the culture and our ordinary mind might say. The truth of our nature is that we are complete. We are beautiful. We lack nothing. We are souls of love unfolding. It is only because we have this deep sense of Reality that we recognize our ordinary self's relentless drivenness as somehow misguided.

Without consciously knowing it, we have encountered Holy Mystery, which is boundless love forever unfolding. We have tasted, touched, heard, smelled something extraordinary in an utterly ordinary encounter. A traditional word for this encounter is *sacrament*. Life is pregnant with love since love is the spiritual fabric of Reality. Creation ceaselessly gives birth in and through ordinary acts of intimate care and generosity. Reality is holy because it is always whole. But we don't feel or believe that to be true. We believe our inner critic that we are deficient. But in the recesses of our sense of self there is a soul compass that knows true north. That soul knowledge is what invites us to continue our search. Discovery is about trusting our longing to realize the truth about our nature.

Our heart knows, without knowing, that there is something more to life than surface. This something more is not a *thing* that fills a hole we believe we have. It is not a *thing* that satisfies our dissatisfaction. The *more* is a *less*. The more is the realization, the awakening, to the truth about who and what we are. We need less than we believe because the truth is that we are always already whole. We need less in the sense that to discover what is already true about our soul we need to divest our self of our daily preoccupations and develop a consciousness that is pruned from distraction and more focused.

As we mature, we are slowly realizing there is more to life than being driven to do and accomplish and succeed. There is more to life than winning the admiration of parents and friends, and the accolades of colleagues. There is more to life than our regular stops to fill ourself up from being depleted from the daily grind.

---

terms *awareness* and *consciousness*. "*Awareness* concerns a mental focusing on an object of experience. *Consciousness* refers to the process of being aware that you are aware, or meta-awareness." Stern, *Present Moment*, 123. We can also understand consciousness from within the discipline and practice of spirituality as the space in which phenomena arise. In other words, "consciousness is not anything itself, just the degree of openness or emptiness, the clearing in which the phenomena of the various lines [of development] appear." Wilber, *Integral Spirituality*, 66. The context will make clear how the terms are being used.

Christ Heart

Our early encounters with being touched—being graced—by someone's love, or some creature's beauty, draw forth our heart to begin the spiritual journey. We want to discover the Source of our self. We want the moon to press her face once more upon us.[4] We want to drink in those azure waters of sky and sea so that they fill every pore and touch every cell of our soul. We want to flow as easily as a river to the sea, nurturing and caressing all in its path.

We long to discover as conscious adults, to know with an awake heart, that we are beloved; *we* are the spiritual fabric of Reality. A discovery that allows the encrusted layers of deficiency, shame, guilt to fall away like exhausted autumn leaves.

When Jesus makes his way down to the Jordan River, allowing John to bathe his body in those living waters (Mark 1:9–11), his journey is the human sojourn of the heart to discover the Source of our life. I don't know when he was touched as a boy by the eyes or hands or voice of love. Maybe he received kindness in the eyes of Mary, a river of love coursing through the difficult life of being a Jewish boy of unknown paternity. Maybe there was an uncle or aunt or village elder who took him under their wing. We don't know. But there was an early encounter, or encounters, with love that held his heart and beckoned it forth.

Jordan is Jesus's discovery of Holy Mystery. What is your Jordan, or Jordans? It's important for us to identify and appreciate our discovery of love—boundless and unfolding love. Maybe it was when a friend stood with you without question during your divorce? Maybe it was during a walk on the beach at dusk alone? Maybe in the tears of loss of a partner? Maybe at an open-air concert as a lone note of the oboe lighted upon your breast? Maybe as you stood side by side to thwart the construction of an oil pipeline?

When we discover Holy Mystery, we begin to truly awaken from our slumber. We are beyond a nonconscious[5] fleeting encounter. We are standing in the river of life with our heart open. We are vulnerable, soft, receiving with our soul what life is giving in the moment. We are aware of the ordinary being pregnant with the extraordinary simply as it is.

The question that now arises is how shall we *live* with Holy Mystery in the next moment?

---

4. Rumi, "There Is Some Kiss We Want."

5. Daniel Stern clarifies that the "term 'unconscious' should be reserved for repressed material where there is a defensive barrier to entering consciousness." With the nonconscious there is no repression at play, rather a lack of explicit awareness. Stern, *Present Moment*, 116.

Part One: Awakening

LIVING WITH HOLY MYSTERY

In discovering Holy Mystery, we are not finding some thing, but realizing the truth about our nature. This discovery is more than a passing experience, but it does flow from an actual experience of being touched by the grace of love in an ordinary encounter. What arises from the experience, marking it as a discovery, is that consciousness is transformed.

We are becoming aware of what we are: boundless love is the Source of life and the longing of the soul. As we live from the Source, we become more curious about life, which means we question, ceaselessly. The questions arise from the desire to know Holy Mystery more fully. But Holy Mystery is an inexhaustive reality: the Deep that calls to our own deep[6] and draws us forward and inward in curiosity about the nature of the soul. There is always more for the heart to know because the Beloved is boundless. Intimacy is infinite.

Once the heart discovers Holy Mystery, the spiritual journey commences in earnest. Consciousness begins to awaken. Discovery, though sweet, draws us forward to taste more. We have stumbled, in part, upon the soul's treasure. If we are steadfast and find a spiritual guide, discovery can mature into learning to live with Holy Mystery.

The soul's treasure is not an ordinary object. Holy Mystery is not a thing we possess like other things in our life. The *object* we have been taught by conventional religion to seek as the source of our salvation (as some one or some thing or some teaching or some doctrine or some belief or some ritual), we realize, is not *out there* but resides in our heart. True, the object is not some ordinary thing, but our own true nature, but this is at first a quite faint awareness. We continue for some time to experience a distance between our heart and its intimate treasure of the Beloved. There is still an object relation, even if it be *I* and *Thou*.

Living with Holy Mystery is the spiritual schooling of the soul. Soulful awakening is an embodied awakening. Learning to live with Holy Mystery is applying all our will to creating a way of life that supports, nurtures, and expresses the boundless love that is us.

The personality is characterized by habitual perceptions, preferences, dislikes, defenses, aversions, passions. The ordinary self is the result of habitual reactions that are relatively consistent over decades. If the discovery of Holy Mystery is to mature into a living with Holy Mystery, then we will need to develop new soulful practices that nurture maturation.

6. I draw upon the wisdom of Ps 42 for this language of the Deep.

This spiritual path is a journey of love; a journey of learning the practices, the ways, and the language of love. It is so easy for spirituality to become lost in the maze of extraordinary experiences or states or esoteric knowledge. All of this can be quite seductive.

Living with Holy Mystery is much simpler and simultaneously asks much more of us. We are being invited to trust so that the grip which fear has on the heart might begin to loosen and release. We are being asked to learn to let go, but the letting go only comes as we understand the power and place of fear in our life. Acknowledging and feeling fear will create the space within for courageous trust to arise.

In the wise and straightforward words of the Buddhist teacher Jack Kornfield I am describing a Christian spiritual path that is a path with heart.[7] Even more, we are exploring the spiritual path of Christ heart as a path *of* heart.

Living with Holy Mystery is the painful and courageous journey of realizing how to be a person of trust, and in turn becoming someone who can relax, enjoy, and be playfully and sensually creative. This is the ancient meaning of *eros*. A heart at rest is thus an erotic heart from which spontaneous creativity flows. Holy Mystery is an erotic spontaneous unfolding of heart.[8]

But how do we learn to live with Holy Mystery? We have welcomed a new lover and they are a stranger in so many ways.

We begin with commitment. We reprioritize daily life, often gradually at first, remaining within our window of toleration so we don't bolt from feeling overwhelmed. We place our love, our dear one, at the center.

The etymology of commitment is to *entrust*. We are handing over the keys to our heart to our lover. We are welcoming our lover into all dimensions of our life. This Beloved is not a weekend tryst or a passing fancy. We are consciously choosing to reorient our life so that the Beloved remains present. When we arise in the morning the Beloved is there. When we lay down to sleep, their heart lies upon ours.

Living with our lover takes practice. Not perfection! Practice. We need practices that engage heart, mind, and body. Holy Mystery is a Beloved ready to receive all of us, not just pieces or parts. Through diligent practice, habits—the ingrained reactiveness of our habitual self—can begin dissolving.

The spiritual path requires core practices capable of reforming (or in biblical language, transfiguring) our life. These are the practices of

---

7. Kornfield, *Path with Heart*.
8. See Almaas and Johnson, *Power of Divine Eros*; and Wilber, *Sex, Ecology, Spirituality*.

meditation; spiritual reflection and exploration; breath, body, and movement; and liturgy. There are others. But these ancient wisdom practices can develop the capacity of the heart to be a lover. Through them we discover our inherent beauty, innate goodness, erotic power, boundless curiosity, primordial unity with creation, and the infinite capacity of the heart to love because the heart's true nature is love.

Meditation

The spiritual path of awakening as Holy Mystery is not primarily a meditative path, but a path of awakening in which meditation is integral. This distinguishes the realization of Christ heart from Buddhism or other spiritual traditions in which meditation is the principal practice. Meditation has a central place in awakening as Holy Mystery. It is pivotal to awakening the heart from its slumber. To be effective, meditation must be consistent, sincere, and practiced with skill. We need a realized teacher as a guide. There are many kinds of meditation. The key is to find that practice that works for you. Be willing to explore several forms and trust your heart. But settle on a form of meditation and stick with it as a daily practice. Meditation teaches how to be with life as it arises. Meditation teaches how to see and let pass the many thoughts and feelings and sensations that arise. Meditation teaches the mind, heart, and body to settle and become grounded. We learn not to run, nor to advance, but to receive—which is to trust Reality.

Spiritual Reflection and Exploration

Human beings are naturally curious, but it is a curiosity dampened by fear. Spiritual reflection and exploration are rekindling the heart's natural desire to ask questions. In spiritual exploration we read, we reflect, we journal, we gather with others to explore. The practice of spiritual reflection and exploration recognizes that we are cultural and social persons, situated within specific worlds of meaning. The implication is that we have prejudices (i.e., unfounded judgments) we don't suspect, blind spots we don't recognize, fears we assume as given.[9] This exploration thus includes and

---

9. The postmodern work of philosopher Michel Foucault highlights that our personal world is inherently an interpersonal world. What this means for spirituality is that any personal awakening will need to critically engage culture, society, and language, otherwise personal bias, ignorance, etc., will remain as determining unconscious forces. See

transcends the field of spirituality per se, recognizing that the holy Source is the origin, or Spirit, infusing all that is. Each scientific discipline—such as developmental psychology, hermeneutics, neuroscience, sociology, systems theory—offers a perspective of Reality that the awakening soul needs to digest. We mature through inquiry and conversation. We are discovering a fundamental truth about Reality: there is never a final answer because there is never a final question. We question because we realize that Reality is a lover that enjoys being intimately explored. Intimacy is infinite.

Breath, Body, Movement

The spiritual teacher Gurdjieff describes most human beings as having become mechanical.[10] Decades of habitual reactivity results in becoming numb to inner life and acting stiffly and routinely without spontaneous connection with heart and body. Hence, his own work integrated movement and dance. Developing a regular practice of breath, body, and movement is integral to awakening as Christ heart. Diamond Body Work[11] is one such practice that I've found to be quite valuable. Christianity *speaks* about incarnation but has forgotten much of its practical wisdom about the body, the breath, and movement. Tai Chi, Reiki, and Dances of Universal Peace are some of the wonderful practices that can develop the erotic sense of breath, body, and movement.

Liturgy

The ancient language says we are the body of Christ. The *we*, however, includes more than human beings. *Reality* is the body of Christ. In liturgy (which, as we shall discover, can be expressed both individually and communally), we offer creative ritual expression about the truth of what we are and what we are experiencing in this moment as the body. In liturgy we are living with Holy Mystery embodied as ritual—embodied in our loss, in our dreams, in our loves, in our hopes, in our anger, in our bewilderment, in our desolation, in our longing. There is no end to the shape ritual may

---

the excellent analyses of Ken Wilber in *Integral Spirituality*, 48; and *Integral Psychology*, 70–73.

10. See Gurdjieff, *Beelzebub's Tales*; and *Life Is Real*.

11. Information about Diamond Body Work can be found at The Diamond Approach Online (online.diamondapproach.org).

take as the expression of the community's devoted heart in the moment. We gather in a town square after a mass shooting to light candles, interlock arms, sing and sway, cry and pray. We sit before a photo of our grandparent on a windowsill at home, perhaps bowing in gratefulness. Liturgy sustains, nurtures, teaches, and encourages us to continue maturing into our living as Holy Mystery, and to surrender all that we are into lives of devotion to the Beloved.

Prayer

I need to add one more practice, which is the breath (*ruha*, in Aramaic) inspiring all the others: personal prayer. Personal prayer is a form of liturgy, as we will discover. Prayer is the heart's conversation with its true love. In the Semitic tradition of Jesus, the heart is the center of the human being; the divine channel for the breath flowing into us from *Alaha*.[12] The heart, cradled by an intricate neural network, guides our spiritual unfolding. Prayer is essentially the heart's musings, cries, bewilderments, longings, wonderments, songs, pleas, and so much more. (Part 4 is dedicated to personal prayers and psalms.)

To discover and live with Holy Mystery is to appreciate the unity of all creatures, because all creatures are living words of the Beloved. Learning to live with Holy Mystery is also a deepening of compassion and love for all that is; a life of restorative justice. Our compassion is not because of an imposed command but because the heart recognizes and responds to the inherent beauty and goodness of creation. Living with Holy Mystery engages us fully in the unfolding of life. Any suffering is everyone's suffering and evokes a response to restore wholeness as best we can. Living with Holy Mystery is loving the Beloved, a Beloved embodied as the infinite beauty of creation and responding with lives that are restorative in word and touch.

Living with Holy Mystery moves the heart to wonder and question whether the union it knows can deepen still further.

---

12. In his beautiful book *Revelations of the Aramaic Jesus*, 16, Neil Douglas-Klotz's exploration touches on this mystery of Reality. He writes that "while *Alaha* is usually translated as *God*, the word derives from Semitic roots meaning both 'yes' and 'no': it relates being and nothingness as part of a greater unity."

AWAKENING AS HOLY MYSTERY

Living *with* Holy Mystery is the spiritual schooling of the soul. The method of this schooling is the spiritual practices that teach us how to become embodiments of the Source: meditation; spiritual reflection and exploration; breath, body, and movement; and liturgy. These are the practices that begin to reground and recenter our life in Holy Mystery: they invite and enable consciousness to be transformed.

These practices, however, are not conventional behaviors. To describe them as practices is a bit misleading. They are not acts we engage in to obtain a desired object. These practices are really non-practices. When taken up as a part of the spiritual journey, they are non-doings. They are ancient wisdom non-practices that reorient the self away from the acquisition of an object. For example, in concentration meditation the mind is learning to let go of conventional objects as we intentionally focus awareness on the breath, suffering, goodness. In non-concentration meditation we simply sit as Reality arises and falls away. These are non-practices because they involve no conventional goal, reorient consciousness, and teach how to rest receptively in the moment.

The predominant affect that often characterizes the discovery of and living with Holy Mystery is *longing*. We initially long to discover that object that will bring us hoped for peace, rest, value. But what we discover is that the Beloved is not the kind of object we presumed it would be. We awaken to the presence of Holy Mystery as the Beloved who dwells in our heart. The spiritual practices are the art of becoming the lover of the Beloved. They intentionally refocus our awareness on Holy Mystery as the Source of our life each moment. The practices are the expression of intimacy itself. Each moment of practice is love actualizing.

From the beginning, the experience of longing fuels our soul's continual search and unfoldment. However, as practice continues and love deepens, what arises is a consciousness that the longing is for more than the heart of my heart, or center of my center. We simply long for more—or less—than a living with Holy Mystery. Augustine (influenced by Plotinus) is right to say that our heart is restless until it finds rest in thee.[13] But there is more—or less—than that. What we can begin to sense is that we've become habituated to our sense of longing. We long to long; that's how we know we

---

13. Augustine, *Confessions* 1:1.

are on the journey. And yet the longing itself is exhausting. The more we long the less peace we know.

So long as Holy Mystery remains a pursued object—even as the Beloved of the heart—the soul experiences a gap that the feeling of longing intimates can be closed. And so the heart comes to spiritual practice with the hope of having a spiritual experience, indicated by the feeling of longing itself, that might temporarily close the gap and relieve the longing.

In awakening *as* Holy Mystery we are realizing that the belief in an object is less and less compelling and the feeling of longing is less and less satisfying. To our surprise, we become aware that Holy Mystery is neither some thing out there nor in here. Holy Mystery is the Reality of our life. Holy Mystery is the land of our soul. We are the land of promise in our very soul. The prior journey of learning to live *with* Holy Mystery is transformed into the journey of living *as* Holy Mystery. The Beloved is a Thou without distance because love is the very truth of our own nature.

The peace that passes all (conventional) understanding, as Scripture says (Phil 4:7), arises as our way of life. In this awakening the soul is at rest because there is no place to go and no thing to obtain—thus, no need to long. The heart is a spacious and still peace even when expressing as erotic creativity. The awakening is the realization that there is no gap, no object, and no ordinary self. The true self is simply a human being that *is* Holy Mystery arising here in this moment. This is awakening as Christ heart. A heart of love loving the Beloved as the Beloved.

We awaken to the gracious truth that the Source—Holy Mystery—is our own true nature. Reality is Holy Mystery graciously arising, or manifesting, each moment as the spirit of everything that is. I say *graciously* because Reality, as it is, is a gift. There is nothing to earn or merit or deserve. We learn to receive what is always already present.

Buddhism speaks of expending all effort to get to the longed-for far shore where we will know enlightenment. We will find ourself upon a shore completely unlike the one from which we first departed. When we finally do arrive on that *distant* shore after investing blood, sweat, and tears, however, we discover we are on the original shore. But our consciousness, our perspective, of what the shore is has been completely transformed. In biblical language, we've crossed over—after years of searching in the desert—into the promised land. And the promised land is the very land of our soul.

In awakening we are discovering that our true nature has always been Holy Mystery. But we did not know this. We were convinced of our inherent deficiency or weighed down by a mistaken sense of guilt and shame or immobilized by the feeling of inadequacy. Conventional religion distorts the spiritual journey into a struggle for salvation from damnation and a rescue into a heaven. The real spiritual journey is our discovery that the truth of our nature is graceful beauty. We are each a pearl beyond price. Our life is the task of discovering that truth by seeing through false beliefs about what we are and knowing directly for ourself the gracious truth of our nature.

In awakening as Holy Mystery we realize the true nature of Reality. Our curiosity continues but our exploration is no longer driven by a sense of fear and deficiency. We are lovers being drawn ever deeper into intimacy with the Source. Reality is a Mystery because the intimacy is infinite. Love forever deepens. Because the Mystery is boundless love, Reality is holy. Our heart is in awe of the innate goodness and inherent beauty of Reality. We are now awake to the truth that love is the spiritual fabric of Reality.

The ordinary self only awakens through spiritual practices that enable it to gradually understand in the heart and body its own inherent beauty. Each practice, engaged with sincerity and skill, slowly dissolves the layers of crust constituted by habitual defenses, avoidances, passions. The spiritual path is not about getting to some place but awakening to the truth that our very soul is the *place* where Holy Mystery is graciously arising now. And the same is true for every other creature that exists. We—all creatures—are the body of Christ, which is the body of Holy Mystery that is Reality.

Part One: Awakening

EXPLORATIONS

1. It is important, vital really, to acknowledge the needs, losses, and defenses we have. Our spiritual growth occurs through exploring—with kindness and tenderness for our self—and understanding through feeling into our self. It is helpful to begin exploring by becoming curious about what feels right to you about feeling driven to do, succeed, perform. We can tend to judge ourself for such ordinary feelings. We want to learn how to acknowledge and honor and hold whatever feelings we have. They are present for a reason. Acknowledging and honoring our feelings gives them and us room to breathe. Only after we have begun to develop a holding space for these feelings can we then ask ourself a following question: How is there more to life for you than being driven to do, succeed, perform? There is no right or wrong response to this question. It may be that you don't feel there is more to life than being driven to do and succeed. If that's the case, honor where your heart is. We are exploring the truth of your present experience, whatever that may be.

2. Was there an early experience of boundless love in your life, your Jordan? What was it and how did it begin to awaken your self, your soul? Describe your experience in as much detail as possible. If you do not recall an experience, what does arise in your heart? What are your feelings?

3. In what ways do you feel less than whole, less than complete? What feels right about feeling less than whole, less than complete?

4. How do you welcome the Beloved into your heart? What spiritual practices support your soul and soften your heart to be receptive?

5. In what ways do you feel whole and complete?

Reflection 2

Christianity as a Nondual Spiritual Path

I AM WHO I AM.

EXOD 3:14

Because you have made us and drawn us to yourself,
and our heart is unquiet until it rests in you.

AUGUSTINE, *THE CONFESSIONS*

God's ground is the soul's ground is *one* ground.

THE MYSTICAL THOUGHT OF MEISTER ECKHART[1]

HOLY MYSTERY IS BOTH emptiness and form, absence and presence, unmanifest and manifest, silence and word, nonbeing and being.[2] These are

---

1. Two excellent resources on Meister Eckhart: McGinn, *Mystical Thought of Meister Eckhart*; O'Neal, *Meister Eckhart, from Whom God Hid Nothing*.
2. Remember we noted above that "while *Alaha* is usually translated as *God*, the word derives from Semitic roots meaning both 'yes' and 'no': it relates being and nothingness

two dimensions of one Reality, which is Holy Mystery. These dimensions are not in opposition, neither are they simply side by side (both one and the other). They are two distinct ways we experience the one mystery of Reality. A common misunderstanding is that emptiness implies a vacuum. The truth is that emptiness exists as Reality in a way different than form. We need to learn this different perspective of Reality, this dimension of emptiness. In Eastern spirituality, the focus of awakening is most often on the realization of emptiness, unmanifest, silence, and nonbeing. In the West, by contrast, attention has predominately centered on form, presence, manifest, word, and being. However, predominate does not mean exclusive, and there are Christian voices that experience the emptiness and speak from the silence. Both dimensions are integral to spiritual awakening and Christ heart.

When we focus on Holy Mystery as *Mystery* we are tending to the dimension of Reality that is emptiness, absence, unmanifest, silence, nonbeing. We are delving into the mystery of love's origin in the emptiness of Reality as well as its rest as absolute silence. When we focus on Holy Mystery as *Holy* our attention turns to the dimension of form, presence, manifest, word, being—all the wondrous embodiments of love that are Reality in its abundance. And this, too, is Reality—the unfolding of life.

Holy Mystery is Source and Manifestation of all: emptiness and form, absence and presence, unmanifest and manifest, silence and word, nonbeing and being. To discover the wonder of our existence as the palpable presence manifesting all existence, that is the realization that dawns in Western spirituality in the story of Moses (Exod 3). Here lies the fountainhead of the later Christian sacramental vision of Reality, where every creature is appreciated as a glimmering forth, a manifesting form, of Holy Mystery. Moses is the touchstone.[3]

---

as part of a greater unity." Douglas-Klotz, *Revelations of the Aramaic Jesus*, 16.

3. Two developmental frameworks for understanding both personal and cultural spiritual development are those of Jean Gebser's worldviews outlined in *Ever-Present Origin* (archaic, magic, mythic, rational, pluralistic, integral) and Don Beck and Christopher Cowan's *Spiral Dynamics* (survivalist, magic, warrior, authoritarian, strategic, egalitarian, integrative, holistic). If we situate the story of Moses in Genesis along these unfolding developmental lines, then the community is within the magic/mythic and magic/warrior stages of these systems. Life is structured around powerful myths about creation and redemption and populated with persons and gods with magical powers. YHWH, the object within Moses's consciousness in Genesis, is a warrior God, a tribal deity, who is feared and revered because of the capacity to set the tribes free from enslavement and thereby begin to make of them a people with a distinct Semitic identity. All this being true, the story contains spiritual significance for us today because we can discover

Christianity as a Nondual Spiritual Path

As Moses climbs the mountain, he arrives at his soul's summit out of breath, bone weary, and hungry—hungry to know the truth of what it is he searches for. He is an embodiment of humanity's search for Reality. Lungs burning and on fire from the exertion, he is bent over in exhaustion and gasping for air to fill his body and satisfy his pounding heart. Alone on the mountain he breathes and breathes and breathes. Slowly the awareness begins to arise—not from above and not from out of the blue—but from within his own hungry breathing and pulsating body; with each breath in and with each breath out, consciousness clears and, ever so gradually, he becomes aware of a new perspective of what is fundamentally true about him: *I am who I am. I am*—he breaths in; *who I am*—he breaths out. Over and over again. Each breath is new, and yet each reveals the same abiding truth: *I am*—he breaths in; *who I am*—he breaths out.

In and through Moses we have perhaps the most pivotal Jewish experience, and thus revelation, in the Hebrew Scriptures. The ground of reality, which is the ground of God and the ground of Moses (which means your ground and my ground), is *I am who I am*, and it arrives on the breath of Moses. The heart that is Moses (who symbolizes all creatures)—pulsating as life with each breath—is arising as Reality in this very moment. Being—which is one way of speaking about how Holy Mystery manifests—is the boundless beauty of all that is. Everything that exists is expressing the same Being that is Holy Mystery. What this story does not explore, at least explicitly, is that this expressive boundless beauty arises from the fathomless deep, silent, unmanifest emptiness that is the font from which flows forth the nondual spiritual path within Christianity.

And this boundless ocean of Holy Mystery that is you, me, the sunflower, the speck of sand, the jackal, the butterfly, is a shoreless sea of love. From this perspective, Holy Mystery is the flow of loving Spirit that by its very nature is without division or separation. To be sure, there are infinite distinctions within this shoreless sea, but no separations. Moses is distinct from YHWH, but YHWH expresses as Moses. The primordial waters give rise to an infinite variety of waves, but each and every ripple embodies and

---

further meaning. We can interpret Moses's encounter as one not only with God as an *object out there*, but with the Mystery of the Holy that is constitutive to his own soul, and every soul. Moses's story, in other words, is paradigmatic for human beings as we seek to understand who we are as we unfold in this life. The beauty and gift of classical texts and stories is that they are pregnant with an abundance of possible meanings with perennial relevance for us to explore. In fact, that is what contributes to their designation as being classical. See Ricoeur, *Hermeneutics and the Human Sciences*, 1981.

expresses the empty boundless water. Moses, or you, or me, could never exhaust the Reality of YHWH; but YHWH is the Reality of Moses, you, and me. Such is the nature of grace. Every creature speaks to the infinite beauty of Reality, which is to say that every creature is a word of Holy Mystery, or a sacrament (to use the traditional Christian language). In every thing we encounter we can taste, smell, touch, see, hear, or simply sense with our soul the presence of Being (and even nonbeing). There is no gap or distance, but an integral intimacy.

Nonduality is not a term original to Jewish, Christian, or Muslim spirituality. However, nonduality captures beautifully and accurately the abiding truth of which I'm speaking and of which Eckhart's perspective intimates when he declared without ambiguity that "God's ground is my ground, and my ground is God's ground."[4] In all its poetic earthiness, *ground* is not really a thing, or an it. Eckhart was searching within the budding German vocabulary he himself was helping to create to give adequate voice to his experience and understanding. Beyond God, he said, was Godhead—that mystery into which all disappears and from which all that is flows. *Godhead* was Eckhart's way of trying to describe the mystery of the dimensions of emptiness, unmanifest, silence and nonbeing that is the Source of boundless oceanic Reality, which is indivisible and from which all spontaneously arises moment to moment.

The importance of realizing Christianity as a nondual spiritual path is that it frees us to continue our natural maturation in Spirit by honoring, attending to, and coming to understand the actual experiences of this life. We acquire a perspective that allows us to appreciate qualities such as compassion, strength, and peace as of the spiritual fabric of our life. Perhaps above all we can discover the freedom of being alone as our self because we no longer search out there for something else to save us from our true self. We are always already of Being. We are never not Holy Mystery self-expressing—which means each and every creature is a sacrament, or a sensible embodiment of boundless love.

Our longing, therefore, is even deeper than that expressed in the heartful cry of Augustine. For with Augustine, God, however beautiful and potentially satisfying, remains an *object* of desire. It really doesn't matter if the object be far or near, it remains an object. For Augustine, and much of the West that lives and thinks in the wake of his theology, God remains a holy object—which is to say, an *it*—not only distinct from, but separate

---

4. Eckhart, Pr. 5b (DW 1:90.8–9), in McGinn, *Mystical Thought*, 45ff, 161.

from, us and all creation. Creator and creation, emptiness and form, remain *essentially* different, disparate, realities. The manifest is severed from, and extrinsic to, the unmanifest. There is a cleft within Reality.

But the soul longs for the most intimate truth of who she essentially is: the Ground manifesting as her Reality. She and Holy Mystery are one, not two. She longs to perceive this truth of her own nature immediately and directly. She is a wave—beautiful and unrepeatable—of boundless Ocean. She is a word whispered from the silent Deep. She is grace. This experience wherein we taste the truth of our origin and of our true nature—which is the budding realization of Moses on the mountain—alone satisfies the hungry heart and is the true meaning of *faith*. Faith is our personal and direct experience of what is really real. Faith is our taste of the water of Spirit of Being that is life itself. Faith then draws the soul forth in growth to realize ever more fully in her life—in all that she does—this truth of who she is.

We can appreciate the richness of the spiritual path of Christianity as being both nondual and what I would describe as transtheistic. Christianity is nondual because there is an integral intimacy that matures without end at the center of Reality. Theism is rooted in separation between emptiness and form, absence and presence, unmanifest and manifest, silence and word, nonbeing and being. Christianity is transtheistic because it can embrace *and* transcend conventional theism; I see no need to discard or devalue conventional theism. Transtheistic is a fuller perspective, as it both includes and transcends.

Christianity's own origin contains an evolutionary thrust propelling it beyond theism, beyond a God who is an object. When the Jesus of John's Gospel exclaims that "I and the Father are one" (John 10:30), this is an epiphany of the heart. The heart of Jesus and the heart of his Abba are of one Ground, one Reality. Jesus is a beautiful Jewish wave of the ocean of Being, a unique word of Holy Mystery. But the Gospel of Thomas pleads with us to realize that what is true of Jesus is true of every human being. Indeed, every creature is a word arising from the Deep. The realization of the truth of who we are by its nature dissolves God as an object of belief. We begin to realize that the very term *God* is best understood and utilized as a poetic way for speaking of the boundlessly gracious quality, which is to say the loving giftedness, of the very fabric of life—Holy Mystery.

Christianity as a nondual spiritual path has far reaching ramifications. Let me briefly note one. For liturgical Christian traditions, like my own, a period such as Lent is transformed into a season of transfiguration much like that enjoined by the nondual mystics (or Hesychasts) of the Orthodox tradition. We are all too often held in bondage by our belief in a divinity who is other—held hostage in our ritual, our prayer, our song. Lent, however, can be a season of healthy spiritual purification, which has nothing to do with puritanical morality, but with soulful clarifying. Eckhart implores us to let go of all our concepts and language about God because they become fixations and idols of the mind. In the language of Buddhism, we get lost in the land of forms divorced from emptiness. Within a nondual Christian spirituality, Lent holds the possibility of being transformed into a seasonal reminder calling us to return to the liquid land of our soul—a land flowing easily upon the river's breath of the truth that I am who I am.

EXPLORATIONS

1. How is your life a spiritual climb? What does your heart burn for?

2. How does it feel that your name is *I am*?

3. If you are not in need of a savior to keep you from judgment, how do you feel?

4. The Gospel of Thomas pleads with us to realize that what is true of Jesus is true of every human being. Every creature is a word arising from the Deep. How does the wisdom of these words land upon your soul? What if the very term *God* is best understood and utilized as a poetic way for speaking of the boundlessly gracious quality, which is to say the loving giftedness, of the very fabric of life—Holy Mystery? When you sense into your heart what fabric do you feel present? Allow yourself time to heartfully investigate.

5. Explore your heart's response to the truth that God's ground and your ground are one ground: no separation.

Reflection 3

Meditation Through the Wisdom of Eckhart

Here,
the core of God is also my core;
and the core of my soul, the core of God's
and here,
I am independent as God himself is independent.

MEISTER ECKHART, FROM *WHOM GOD HID NOTHING*

SPIRITUALITY AND POLITICS ARE integrally related. I don't mean partisan politics, as in Democrat or Republican. I am referring to the classical meaning of the word. Human beings are gregarious creatures who form societies and develop systems that promote the common sense of value they perceive as embodying what is good (this is the basic meaning of culture). All too often spirituality and politics are seen as separate and unconnected (a product of the radical Enlightenment), or unilaterally determinative (such as we see in right-wing Evangelical Christianity or reactionary Roman Catholicism, where a particular spirituality or belief system requires a specific partisan political position). I am speaking of an integral relationship much more complex, basic, and significant.[1]

COMMON GROUND

Democracy is only able to function and prosper if its diverse citizenry shares a *common* perspective of what values constitute the good that everyone shares. A political *common good*, however, is only possible because of a deeper dimension of Reality we all share, which is the *common ground*. This ground is common because the ground is Holy Mystery. Common, whether it refers to *good* or *ground*, reflects the true nature we all share as expressions of Being. This Reality of a common ground makes it possible for human beings to discover and nurture a common good of shared values. These shared values constitute the core of a cultural and political common good. This ground is common because it is the Being we all share. Common ground is the true nature of existence, although most of us neither directly experience this truth nor know it.

Our spiritual perspective of shared ground makes possible the appreciation of each person as an embodiment of Holy Mystery; makes possible for human beings to discover and nurture a common good of shared values. These shared values constitute the core of a cultural and political common good. Spiritually, when we take this a step deeper, we discover that the ground we share underpinning whatever degree of common good we know has always already been present as a real potential of the human condition. From this perspective, ultimately ground is common and hallowed because love is the Source from which every creature arises. Without spiritual realization of Reality's common ground, however, the fragile political common good is particularly precarious and ephemeral, evident in the cultural blindness to and destruction of the beauty of someone such as George Floyd. The cultural narrative of racism does not recognize his existence as expressive of a common ground, nor behold his presence as a beauty to be valued as a common good.

As I said, ground and good, spirituality and politics, are integrally related—Being is the Source (without determining any specific outcome, which would be fundamentalism). Within modernity, however, they are seen as separate and unconnected. Yet the ground, or Being, makes the

---

1. For a comprehensive analysis of the making of our modern identity see Taylor, *Sources of the Self.*

good possible. But there are so many shapes the good can take. By saying the ground and the good are integrally related doesn't mean to imply the relationship is simplistic. The good takes myriad forms, as various peoples within various cultures undertake their journey to a shared sense of what distinct expressions of the good is common for them.

The focus for us here is that without our realization of the common ground, the common good (whatever culturally distinct form may take) is particularly fragile because it lacks grounding depth. Holy Mystery expressing as personal spirituality and maturing into commonly held understandings of communal faith is integral to the human capacity to create body politics and social systems that revere, support, and encourage human development and flourishing. Human beings, as our Greek and Roman ancestors discovered, are inherently political creatures, living and working and playing together. And to live together in any semblance of harmony we must engage in continual dialogue as the process necessary to forge those common values around which we function. All interpersonal dialogue is a dialogue between persons, which means it is spiritual conversation. We are restless, whatever common good we both discover and create together, to the degree that the good we realize does not also fully embody our pearly possibility as persons of Being. And it is also true that since we are historical creatures there will never be a full and perfect embodiment of the ground in any particular good—every culture and society are imperfect and with ample room to grow. The human experiment in democracy shall never end.

The spiritual journey impacts political life because the process of realizing our common ground is a dialogical path that radically changes our perspective and thus how we receive ourself and one another. If we don't experience and know the ground of Being—in whatever form Holy Mystery is known by human beings—in its absence, fear blindly drives us to survive, and we destroy beauty misperceived as a threat. Our cultural dialogue is stunted and unwittingly blind.

The challenge of not only appreciating but of living a life that embodies the ground and good as being in a dynamic integral relationship is not new. Scientific knowledge and cultural diversity in the twenty-first century certainly add significant new challenges to the relationship. And yet, we can draw from wisdom to be found in history.

We are going to turn now to a thirteenth- and fourteenth-century wise German teacher, or meister, we met passingly in the previous reflection. During the inquisitorial religious madness of Europe's Dark Ages, the

German mystic and theologian Meister Eckhart perceived with a clarity that continues to speak to us today. In the prevailing culture, God was experienced as a distant moral judge condemning the bulk of creation. In stark contrast, Eckhart intimately experienced the Godhead, realizing that its Mystery held and touched all reality as a shoreless sea. "God," he said, "is nearer to me than myself.... He is also near and present for a stone or piece of wood, but they know nothing about this fact."[2] We need to take a few deep breaths, relax, and allow that awareness of Holy Mystery to slowly sink into our heart. God, he kindly whispers to our soul, is near each and every creature, including stones and splinters. Oh, how Christianity has either forgotten or never even known this perspective of Reality.

There are no gaps or absences to the presence of Holy Mystery in life. Moreover, as we shall see, this presence is without judgment, for the presence is of goodness and love itself. We can breathe. Because we can relax. Because there is no one, no thing, to fear. Our defenses can disband. Our bellies can soften. Eckhart is offering a spiritual perspective that has the capacity to transcend that of the magic and mythic worldviews in which the divine judge lives.[3]

Amid pervasive and pandemic institutional fear of women and color and laity—of trust in human experience—Eckhart was courageously developing a new language to express his unfolding perspective of what he called the very *ground* of Reality. His choice of language is so earthy. This earth (creation) is not a fallen mass of depravity. Creation. Nature. All this cosmos is *of* the ground. Eckhart is beginning to understand that Spirit is in the mud as well as the stars, and is the Source. And not simply *in* these

---

2. Eckhart, "Sermon Nine," 137.

3. In footnote 3 on page 18 of reflection 2, I referred to two developmental frameworks for understanding both personal and cultural spiritual development: that of Jean Gebser's *worldviews* (archaic, magic, mythic, rational, pluralistic, integral) and that of Don Beck and Christopher Cowan's *Spiral Dynamics* (survivalist, magic, warrior, authoritarian, strategic, egalitarian, integrative, holistic). If we situate Eckhart within the unfolding spiritual developmental line, unlike Moses/Genesis we can see that he is a person living and functioning within a mythic/rational and authoritarian culture. I believe he is one of those special individuals whose personal spiritual development is pushing the developmental envelope of his culture. God as an object is dissolving into the spiritual Godhead. He is able to acknowledge the inherent limitations of language. His personal unfoldment, hinted at in his own description of and teaching about spirituality, strongly suggests his realization of nonduality. As I said before, the beauty and gift of classical texts and stories is that they are pregnant with an abundance of possible meanings with perennial relevance for us to explore. I am drawing upon Eckhart as a springboard for exploration, not as focus for historical analysis. See Ricoeur, *From Text to Action*.

variations of ground; Being, Holy Mystery, is *embodied as* these realities. Again. There are no gaps where some supposedly divine judge or evil entity lingers. Life is integrally sacramental.

I turn us to Eckhart because he recognizes so clearly that humanity—indeed all creation—embodies and reveals the divine; which is to say, incarnates the divine. Eckhart invites Christianity to transcend the limiting shackles of a dualistic spirituality, with a holy judge on one side and a fallen creation on the other in need of being saved. Eckhart is articulating that the human spiritual path is not to connect a depraved creature with a distant, judgmental God object. No, not at all. We exist so that we might realize that the graciously empty ground of Reality is the eternal Source of every thing, every one, that comes to be.

Here, the word *empty* conveys the truth that Holy Mystery is simply boundless love without any agenda or plans as we commonly understand those words. The ground—Silent Source of our true nature—is this boundless emptiness that mysteriously invites us to be love and to know love. Although there are reasons to interpret this ground Neoplatonically, as a preexisting given to which we are called to return. I would suggest that there are more possibilities, such as appreciating the ground as a groundless ground, or as a way of expressing emptiness, or non-being. This groundless ground is the Source, the infinite womb, of all that arises. There is no thing that is not an expression of this womb. Each and every expression of this womb is a manifestation (i.e., sacrament) of boundless love. When Jesus cries out that he and his Abba are one, he is speaking for all creatures. Each of us is one with Holy Mystery, one as Holy Mystery, only we haven't realized it yet. This realization of the groundless ground as the empty Source of all that is is the spiritual journey.

We long to know in our heart that Holy Mystery is what we are. We are looking for our home. But we are not looking to go back to a lost Eden. We are attending to the ground, so to speak, that is our sense of self at this very moment. And *empty* speaks to the critique of any presumption of having or achieving a spiritual perspective that is completely objective and without any bias; in other words, *empty* is the enduring invitation of Being to ever greater intimacy with Holy Mystery. We continue to discover ways in which our heart withholds; our body contracts; our mind fears. Each is a barrier, however thin it might be, to deepening intimacy with Holy Mystery. We are continually self-emptying (the spiritual thrust of the Greek word *kenosis*), as we understand and release the constraining chains of our historical conditioning. The emptiness we do realize exposes the spiritual clinging to our positions and perspectives which still exists.

A teacher or a teaching exists to nurture this spiritual journey. All too often in religion the teacher or teaching becomes the ground to which we cling for security, rather than the support for further exploration. We become filled with belief and doctrine of a certain perspective that is a poor substitute for the freedom of spiritual emptiness.

This poor substitution occurs repeatedly throughout history. As he surveyed the early fourteenth century Eckhart beheld a church and its piety riddled with this perspective and reinforced with a teaching of a corrupt creation living at a distance from Holy Mystery. This complex and corrosive misunderstanding was a dense fog shrouding medieval life, dulling experience, and blinding recognition of Reality. (So many of us today are heirs of this limited and distorting perspective.) As a member of the Dominican order, Eckhart was a preacher. And unlike the other preachers of his day, he spoke to the laity as well as the clerics. Christianity was full of itself and lost and he knew it.

Eckhart's preaching is ceaseless fire burning through the haze, not only of medieval Europe but of contemporary life. His clear teaching, rooted in his own spiritual life, reflective of his own personal experience of the beautiful goodness of Holy Mystery, kindly holds our heart so that it might be willing to open, awaken, and receive the healing truth that creatures, simply as creatures, are divine. You and I are beautiful and good and valuable.

Eckhart is a wise elder who forges a new spiritual perspective from his own experience and study (and perhaps even from his shared learning with other mystics) that nature is inherently sacred since it is nothing other than the bodying forth of Holy Mystery.[4] That's what each of us is: Holy Mystery uniquely being embodied. This perspective is another way of affirming that life is inherently sacramental. For the transformed heart, the Christic heart, he proclaims "that all things become simply God to you, for in all things you notice and love only God."[5]

As we awaken, we only see Holy Mystery in whatever we do see. The face of each creature we behold is divine beauty. In the face of a hateful and threatening Inquisition, Eckhart is unwavering and crystal clear. All

---

4. "Recent research has made it clear that Eckhart very probably had read Marguerite Porete's *Mirror of Simple Souls*. While the case for direct influence of Hadewich and Mechthild on Eckhart remains questionable (though certainly possible)." McGinn, *Meister Eckhart and the Beguine Mystics*, 3–4; also see *Mystical Thought of Meister Eckhart*.

5. Eckhart, Pr. 103.126–38, quoted in McGinn, *Mystical Thought*, 64.

that is is nothing other than Holy Mystery manifesting. This manifesting is a flowering, empty of all striving and self-absorption. Simple. Beautiful. Enjoyable. Joy is all too often a quality missing from our spiritual life. When our heart is beholding beauty joy is a natural response. We see all creatures as good, deeply good, and we smile and we receive, and perhaps tears of gratitude sparkle upon our face.

Through Eckhart we rediscover a largely forgotten truth about ourselves; or perhaps it is more accurate to say that Christianity and the West are being introduced to a more integrating perspective of Reality. To be a human being is to have a heart longing to know the simple truth, or ground, of our own nature. Recognizing, respecting, and courageously tending to this longing is the authentic human life, which is nothing other than the mystical life in which we are awakening as Holy Mystery. We undertake our human journey only to gradually discover that we are blessed from the beginning not by being *of* Holy Mystery. There is no distance, no gap, between Holy Mystery and us. This is why we speak of awakening *as* Holy Mystery. In our spiritual practice we are realizing that our groundless ground is love, and that this love mysteriously unfolds in amazing and surprising ways as our very heart.

Because we are love, we are holy. We are beautiful. We are innately good. We are valuable. Since love is the spiritual fabric of true nature, all is holy. As we slowly awaken to this truth of ourself, we are breaking through the fog of our sleep to know directly—as Eckhart did—*God's ground is my ground, and my ground is God's ground*. We are not believing or accepting this because someone tells us to. The wisdom of tradition certainly guides and supports us, but the whole point of human existence is to realize this truth for ourself. In this discovery is the human realization of our Christic heart that is our true nature.

Eckhart's teaching would launch an entire spiritual renewal in Germany and beyond, even though the church hierarchy tried to silence him. His teaching had, and continues to have, impact because it was rooted in a perspective of experience available to others. Eckhart wasn't speculating about our human condition. He was speaking from his experience as he plumbed the depths of the ground of his soul.

He identifies three threads that intertwine like the braids of a Celtic spiral creating the spiritual path. As we follow this path we penetrate ever deeper and ever wider into the divine common ground until we experience what he describes as a "breakthrough."[6] Our heart is no longer asleep and dull but alive and capable of tasting Reality anew. We taste for ourself—nurtured by the teaching of wise elders but not spoon-fed into belief through doctrine—that every one is nothing but the presence of Holy Mystery. Our heart, our Christ heart, becomes awakened to its capacity to know Holy Mystery. We recognize each creature is Christ and our response is compassionate reception and a restorative justice that lifts and removes the knee pressed down upon any holy one—and every one is a holy one. We are now consciously beginning to live from our common ground and it clarifies for our soul the common good we all share. Our spiritual breakthrough as a maturing Christ heart enables us to see a common ground upon which all may stand with dignity of their true nature. Let's look briefly at Eckhart's three threads of the spiritual life, culling from them wisdom for our journey today.

THREAD ONE: MEDITATION AND LETTING GO

If we are to directly experience the ground of Being, which is boundless love, we must learn to be in silence and stillness. This is because our attention is ordinarily absorbed by the incessant wave of objects exciting our senses. In the stillness, which requires courage for our heart to enter, we learn to allow our wants and desires, our fears and hungers, our many attachments and various identifications, to arise, be seen and pass. This is far from easy, because our instinct is to reach out to grab or to turn away in rejection. This dance of desire and rejection is our ordinary and exhausting reaction to life. We exist unaware of our continual clinging and desiring. There is nothing wrong with our reaction. This is not a matter of right and wrong. Rather, this dance of grasping and rejecting is exhausting and futile and limiting. The soul longs for true sustenance and satisfaction.

Unbeknownst to our ordinary functioning self, the spiritual path often begins in earnest in the silence birthed within meditation. In silence, we begin, awkwardly and uncertainly at first, to turn inward. We intentionally focus our attention, not on the ordinary objects that attract or repel but on nothing but our breath or our belly. Perhaps for the first time in our adult life we experience being alone and quiet with ourself without ordinary distractions. We are allowing our attention to sink below the dimension of the manifest. What we discover is that previously nonconscious distractions

---

6. See McGinn, *Mystical Thought*, 131–47.

Meditation Through the Wisdom of Eckhart

arise and sometimes we encounter barriers from within and from our own unconscious. We are being introduced to new terrain of our self. This can be scary and a new form of suffering as we learn to sit and receive.

In his own way, Eckhart is reminding us that our awakening as Holy Mystery begins with this inward turn, where we learn the skill of awareness and become in touch with our own consciousness. Meditation—introducing us to the reality of silence—of some form is our first step. One that lays the foundation for the arising of Christ heart.

Based on his own experience, as well as his spiritual direction of other women and men, Eckhart recommends a meditation practice—not unlike Zen—in which we learn to let go of images and reactions and passions. Letting go is neither denial nor denigration. We learn to release because these occupying attachments contract consciousness and cause attention to become stuck on transient phenomena. We can become stuck on—merged with—both painful and enjoyable memories, feelings, or sensations. Indeed, creation is so beautiful that we want to possess things forever and never lose them; attention becomes habitually absorbed by minutiae and we miss the subtle presence of (empty) silence and absence and space.[7]

Our heart is discovering how to release what in fact cannot be held. Trying to hold on is inevitably frustrating, like attempting to hold water in a clenched fist. We learn to become aware of the subtle presence of Holy Mystery arising as this spacious (empty) moment. As we become less identified with the desires and revulsions of our personality, gracious space arises. The foreground of mental activity recedes so that the silent ground of Reality may be present to consciousness. This is not a stingy act of suppression but a kind practice of noticing and releasing and relaxing. And it takes patient practice. What is happening is that we slowly become able to relax in and as the space; we search less and less for a particular attractive object to hold onto. We are realizing the dimension of Holy Mystery that is emptiness.

Eckhart says we can be surprised that in letting go we might feel a sense of "poverty," which for many of us is not an attractive condition.[8]

---

7. Each of us has a shadow, the unconscious, where what we don't know and haven't acknowledged has, by definition, not yet been explored, digested, and owned. This is information that was unavailable to Eckhart. Meditation unquestionably assists us with disidentifying with what we have already explored, digested, and owned. However, to the degree we have not explored, digested, and owned what lies within, Ken Wilber observes that disidentifying is double dissociation. Meditation is not a spiritual bypass to necessary psychological work. See Wilber, *Integral Spirituality*, 131–34.

8. See Eckhart, "Sermon Fifteen," 217.

Part One: Awakening

This poverty, at first, is often experienced as a sense of lack or deficiency. We are so used to holding something tight in the fist of our heart. Fullness, not emptiness, is our ordinary sense of self. Now we are holding nothing. Our heart is open. We feel a little dis-ease. Shouldn't there be something occupying and claiming our heart's attention? If we can acknowledge this longing but not act on it, we realize a new freedom in this poverty. There is a peace and quiet from not having to have something. Our mind and heart and body let the craving pass. In Eckhart's perceptive words, "He is a poor person who wills nothing and knows nothing and has nothing." He adds:

> True poverty of spirit consists in keeping oneself so free of God and of all one's works that if God wants to act in the soul, *God himself becomes the place* wherein he wants to act—and this God likes to do.[9]

As our soul becomes empty of ordinary preoccupations, we experience what Buddhism calls emptiness or spaciousness: the soul is as the sky—boundless space with clouds passing through. For Christians, this emptiness is the spacious reality of Holy Mystery; present as the absence of ordinary preoccupations. Presence as absence. Holy Mystery as freeing absence. Here the Silence speaks without voice. Our very soul, our Christ heart, is awakening to being spacious and free Holy Mystery. We enjoy this. We experience rest and freedom and peace. We feel home.

One of our realizations from this direct experience of Holy Mystery is that names and language can clutter. They feel cumbersome and heavy. Eckhart invites us to let our sense of emptiness deepen further, letting go even of *God*. What he means is that our heart grasps for God like any other object. (Remember that ground is a groundless—or empty—ground.) We use all kinds of religious language, and we get lost in our heads. Language seduces us into believing we *know* what Reality is. All the names we have learned to address Holy Mystery get in the way of simply being with Reality and relaxing as Holy Mystery. We forget that *God*, too, is a name, a symbol pointing to Reality beyond the confines of all names. Beyond every name lies the true fullness of Holy Mystery, which Eckhart calls the *Godhead*. The Godhead is Holy Mystery beyond all images and names. Godhead arises as boundless, silent, Holy Ground.

Eckhart is inviting us to a new spiritual perspective. The unfolding spiritual path is not a practice of coming to arrive in the otherness of

---

9. Eckhart, "Sermon Fifteen," 217.

boundless love, but of our self expressing as boundless love. All divisions burned away. The true nature, the groundless ground, of every creature is actually empty, boundless Holy Mystery. Eckhart offers this pearl of wisdom, which invites us to drop beneath the surface of our preoccupations and beyond our perseverating mind into our undivided heart.

> You should love God mindlessly, that is, so that your soul is without mind and free from all mental activities. . . . You should love him as he is, a not-God, not-mind, not-person, not-image—even more, as he is a pure, clear One, separate from all twoness.[10]

THREAD TWO: THE FRUIT OF MEDITATION—BIRTHING

As we develop our capacity to be in silence.

As we become aware of the inner narration of our self that never seems to cease.

As we slowly become able not to become consumed by this inner talk but let it flow.

Each time we intentionally and gently return our awareness to silence and its spaciousness, our familiar self is dissipating (a form of dying), and Christ heart is being born. Within Eckhart's perspective, this phenomenon is understood as *birthing*.

The spiritual life is a continual process of birthing, and meditation is the midwife. Part of the life emerging is our capacity to release what usually captures our attention—our inner narration that tells us what we like and what we don't like, what we want and what we don't want. Each release is a birthing pang, a dissolving of the boundaries of our present sense of self. Our sense of self wants to camp out with what is already familiar and comfortable. We want to enjoy the sense of familiar fullness rather than continue to mature into emptiness. A heart of courage sustains us. In each pang is a small birth, a deepening of our heart's trust in silence; our heart's trust of resting in and flowing as its true nature.

The birthing never ends. The Mystery is that Christ heart never stops maturing. The Mystery is that there is no end state to our spiritual maturation as authentic humans of Being. We never reach a point or state where we dust off our self and say, I'm finished, I'm fully enlightened. The Deep of Holy Mystery is infinite, which means we are infinite. We continue to

---

10. Eckhart, "Sermon Twelve," 180.

discover new identifications, new fixations, new reactions that divide, confuse and fog Reality. We also discover deeper dimensions of boundless love and are continually presented with new frontiers of human knowledge that challenge our embodiment of love.

THREAD THREE: MEDITATION AND BREAKTHROUGH

Although the spiritual path never ceases, there are transitions, which are openings, that are of significance and important to recognize. Eckhart describes one such transition as a *breakthrough*. There are different senses of breaking through that we experience. One kind of breaking through is when we realize we are more than our usual or historic sense of self. Our ordinary machinations seem a little lighter and a little less alluring. We can have a sense that a fog is lifting. A fog we hadn't even perceived before. It's as if we begin to experience a blue expanse of spacious sky. We have discovered Holy Mystery and are being schooled in its ways.

But I need to be clear. We don't break through as if somehow we exert enough effort over a long enough period of time to dispel the fog by conquering our self, controlling our thoughts, dominating our emotions, or denying our body. No. We participate sincerely and steadfastly and wisely in our meditation (as well as our faith exploration, breath and body movement, and liturgy) and the breakthrough happens as grace. The breakthrough is not a reward but the fruit. We sincerely nurture and courageously remain steadfast in our practice of caring for our soul's life. As we do, our heart becomes softer, more vulnerable, more open to the reality of Holy Mystery. The mind quiets, the body relaxes, and the heart's wings unfurl—space arises for Holy Mystery to become known.

We are surprised and grateful, just as an infant is as she reopens her eyes after having been delivered from the womb, with her tiny being kinesthetically entering and expanding into a whole new world. For the child to survive and thrive the truth is that they need to leave the safe harbor of the mother's womb. So, too, must we shed our small, defended self—which served us well in our younger days as we climbed the steep paths of young adulthood—and allow our maturing soul to discover her boundless ground. Birthing is a delivering, which means it involves a dying to a former life and the emergence of a new one.

One of the gifts of meditation is that within its silence and focused attention is the continuous invitation to perceive ever more subtle expressions of our internal dialogue; to recognize ever more tender images we have of ourself; to feel the many ways our heart and body are reactively triggered into fear, anger, envy. Another gift is that we become more sensitive to the limitations of the conventional religious language we use. Our soul is realizing that nothing can contain or control Holy Mystery. The ground is endless. The love is boundless. The birthing continuous. Silence, rather than words, speaks the language of Holy Mystery so much more clearly than words, which can begin to feel heavy and clunky. I am describing how we experience our maturation, which has nothing to do with being right or wrong. We are in a very different field, as Rumi says, beyond the small confines of right and wrong.[11]

Let me switch metaphors. We are beginning to dwell not only in the shoreless silence, but *as* the silence. A silence even present in our speaking. The soul is not trying to achieve anything. She is dying to doing, discovering that meditation is a resting as Spirit, an awakening as Holy Mystery. We come to know the practice of meditation as a kind of non-practice, in that our ordinary agenda and usual preoccupations are not leading the way. Reality is. We are beginning to lose, Eckhart reminds us, our ordinary desires, images, and conventional understandings of who we take ourself to be.[12]

In a spiritual sense we are being stripped of everything we identify with—our job, our gender, our sexual orientation, our many roles. We find this very hard. (We take our sense of fullness for granted.) Our mind can think we are losing our relationships because our various self-identities are dissolving. Who will be relating to whom? What is actually happening is that we are being transformed with a new Christ heart emerging that no longer lives from fear but love. We need to be patient and kind with our soul as Christ heart is being formed. Sometimes growth feels more like death. Slowly, slowly, the *who* we have assumed our self to be is dying. But it is not being buried in some shallow and forgotten grave in the unconscious. Everything that is happening is transpiring within Holy Mystery. Holy Mystery now has the space and freedom to be more fully the living Reality of our being. No longer is it not only true that Holy Mystery is our true nature, but we are also beginning to live lives that embody that truth. The Godhead, in Eckhart's spiritual language, is now living "as no other than itself."[13] Holy Mystery is relating uniquely as us within the world we live.

11. Rumi, "Out beyond ideas of wrongdoing and right doing."
12. Eckhart, "Sermon Fifteen," 217.
13. Eckhart, Jostes 82 (95.28–36), quoted in McGinn, *Mystical Thought*, 146.

Part One: Awakening

Breakthrough involves a fuller perspective of our spiritual unfolding. The soul is realizing her real potential, realizing the promise of her precious, pearly self. That is why the spiritual journey is a process of awakening. The long sleep is over. Our eyes are opening. Christ heart is the fruit of the slow realization of our promise as embodiments of Holy Mystery. The pearl of great price has always been here as our true potential—the real potential of our spiritual maturation; a potential hidden by our preoccupations with so many other things that are not the fullness of who we are or what we seek. That capacity for fullness is already within, waiting to be known and nurtured. Meditation nurtures through the silence; a wisening silence in which we are intentionally learning to let the usual objects in our awareness arise and pass. The complete surprise is that in realizing in our daily life the real potential of boundless love, we are home and we recognize our home. Our heart is full and tender and strong. Our heart is Christ. We have the capacity now to live in the world freely and fully, able to appreciate all this is as a jeweled manifestation of Holy Mystery.

Christ heart receives and lives in this world, this sacred Reality, in a new way. The common ground births a love of, a recognition of, a respect for, the common good. She has begun to know the truth about the nature not only of human beings but of all creatures. All that is arises as the embodiment of the ground, of Holy Mystery. This means Reality as such is sacred. There is nothing profane about the cosmos. Each creature, each human, is an incarnation of Holy Mystery—a sacrament. Most often we do not know that, and we suffer, and we inflict suffering. Not because we are bad but because we are blind.

Christ heart has awakened to a most precious truth: whatever we behold is Holy Mystery beautifully embodied.

EXPLORATIONS

1. What are some of the ways you do not experience Holy Mystery as the common ground of life?

2. What are some of the ways you do experience Holy Mystery as the common ground of life?

3. What is your experience with silence and stillness in meditation? What do you find challenging? What do you find liberating?

4. How do you experience intentionally focusing your awareness in meditation on your breath? Have you tried focusing on your innate goodness, or suffering, or joy? If so, what have you discovered?

5. How do you resonate with the statement that in the spiritual journey and in the practice of meditation *our heart is discovering how to release what in fact cannot be held*?

6. The Mystery is that the Christ heart never stops maturing. Take some time to identify the ways you feel/think that the spiritual journey does have an end. Identify how it might be true for you that the heart never stops maturing.

7. *Spiritual breakthrough is not a reward but a fruit of practice.* How does this statement resonate or not with your experience?

PART TWO

——— Unfolding ———

Reflection 4

Celebrating the Curious Christ Soul

When you come to know yourselves, then you will be known,
and you will realize that you are the children of the Living Father.
If, however, you do not come to know yourselves,
then you dwell in poverty and you are the poverty.

GOSPEL OF THOMAS 3:4–5 *NNT*

[Bodhidharma] was uncompromising in that he wanted to know what was true,
and he wasn't going to take anybody else's word for it.
His big discovery was that by looking directly into our own heart,
we find the awakened Buddha,
the completely unclouded experience of how things are.

CHÖDRÖN, *WHEN THINGS FALL APART*

I am the true vine.

JOHN 15:1

You are no longer a Christian but Christ.

GOSPEL OF PHILIP IN *THE GNOSTIC BIBLE*

Part Two: Unfolding

Once, I was at the department of motor vehicles to get the tags for my motorcycle. As I sat in the chair, with my little numbered paper stub in hand, I noticed out of the corner of my left eye a broad-shouldered person sit down a row behind me. Shoulder length hair, lovely black pantsuit with purple and mauve accents, my sense was that she was a transgender woman. Here we sat in this common public space, in a relatively small and rural midwestern town, early in the morning, needing to transact our personal business.

My number was called, but I was informed I needed to have my insurance company fax a document. I left the counter to make my call and request. Upon my return, the woman in the striking pantsuit was with another attendant. There is not much privacy standing in close quarters at the counter, and so I became aware that she was seeking to have the gender of her driver's license changed. I became very curious, as well as concerned. How would this play out? How would the female attendant respond? How safe was this woman? She had no idea when she had walked into the waiting area a few minutes earlier how she would be seen (if she would be seen) and received (or would it be ridicule and rejection).

I search for words to describe the interaction, but it was simply ordinary—humane and human. A public servant was helping a citizen change the gender of her driver's license so that it might reflect who she knew herself to be. Such a simple and straightforward interaction, and yet nothing about their conversation in that public space, in which the woman was utterly vulnerable and at the mercy of the many she did not know, was simple or straightforward.

I wonder now what this woman's journey has been thus far. In viticulture, for a vine to take root and flourish and produce luscious and juicy fruit requires intense and focused and sustained (we could say, uncompromising) labor. Threats to the vine's health take various forms—from molds to pests to weather to ignorance. Without the wise cultivator, a healthy vine can wither or be mistakenly pruned and killed.

When we are young, our families and various communities are supposed to be present in a way that nurtures our growth. To play with the Gospel of John's metaphor, they are to guide the planting of our soul in rich and loamy soil, watered with the tears of joy and sorrow and loss and hope, so that we might take root and flourish. So that the juices of our soul flow freely and fully. So that we come to enjoy and relish and trust the unfoldment of our soul as sacred and beautiful. We are to be tended so that we ourself—in all our uniqueness—become the precious fruit.

Celebrating the Curious Christ Soul

Who nurtured this woman as a child? Who encouraged her to attend to her mysterious emerging life? When had she first realized the disparity between the culturally expected gender roles laid upon her and her own soul's longings? When had she first realized the disparity between her genitalia, the culturally expected gender roles laid upon her, and her own soul's longings? At what point, like Bodhidharma, had she begun to become uncompromising in wanting to know what was true about her soul and not take anyone else's word for it? When had she begun to realize she was an irreplaceable vine, a Christ coursing with vitality? When had she begun to awaken to the truth that being the poverty of ignorance would be no life?

As Pema Chödrön so poignantly writes, when did she trust herself enough to begin to look directly into her own heart and become her own mother and father to her own birth as a beautiful woman who could one day walk clearly and crisply into the public space of a small, rural, midwestern town, and casually and confidently ask that the gender of her driver's license be changed?

Curiosity. I clearly have no idea when her awakening began to unfold. Yet I was the recipient of her graceful presence. I was witness to the fruit of her unfoldment—unmistakably bold and bright. But the awakening began years before with curiosity within her soul to come to know the truth about her own experience of herself. Might we speak of some kind of uncompromising curiosity to discover the source of her desires? A thirst to know the pulsation and flow of her longings, and the sacred beauty of her wantings, that manifested in the strong and sure, lovely woman—Christ—who conversed with an attendant on an early morning in a midwestern town?

The Gospel of Thomas reminds us, "When you come to know yourselves, then you will be known, and you will realize that you are the children of the Living Father" (Gos. Thom. 3:3 *NNT*). Sooner or later, if we are to realize our Christ heart, we must come to know ourself. No one else can do the knowing for us. But—what a tremendous grace it is when we don't have to ceaselessly contend with supposed faith communities about the sacred fruit we are, nor fear that they desire to prune away our life.

"You are no longer a Christian but Christ."[1] We are not facsimiles; each of us is an original vine of luscious Holy Mystery. We enjoy the taste of our soul when it is relaxed, spacious, creative, spontaneous, joyous, and free. This is the taste of truth—not truth as theory or as abstraction, but truth as a concrete and utterly intimate realization. Thomas, Bodhidharma, John, Philip,

---

1. Barnstone and Meyer, *Gnostic Bible*, 277.

and Pema are all speaking of this journey of realizing our basic humanity, coming to know that the truth of our being is a vine coursing with the very vitality of boundless love. This woman is realizing: I am the vine, I am the soul through which Holy Mystery pulsates with life, my life. My sense is that for her to do the utterly ordinary act of walking into the public space of the department of motor vehicles is an embodiment of uncompromising courage flowing from the uncompromising curiosity of a child—whose desire to live as Christ is now the heart of an amazing woman.

EXPLORATIONS

1. Who nurtured you as a child? How was your body, your mind, your heart seen, tended to, appreciated?
2. When did you begin to awaken and become curious about your own soul? Longing to know the truth of who you are?
3. In what ways does your spiritual community, if you have one, nurture and encourage your soul's unfoldment?

Reflection 5

Dawning of Christ Consciousness

> John the baptizer appeared in the wilderness, proclaiming a baptism of repentance for the forgiveness of sins. . . . And a voice came from heaven, you are my Son, the Beloved; with you I am well pleased.
>
> MARK 1:4, 11

IT IS IMPORTANT FOR us to pause and consider what might be happening in the soul when someone, such as the president of the United Sates, refers to the predominately black countries of Africa and that of Haiti with dehumanizing racist rhetoric? What might be happening to the heart when political leaders seek simplistic solutions to cultural shifts in the erection of separating walls? What is happening to us when the US president fails to condemn neo-Nazi violent demonstrations?

Unacknowledged fear withdraws the soul from intimate contact in the hope that survival is secured through separation. The unattended fearful soul, over time, develops what is described as a schizoid, or split, structure. The self unconsciously pulls back or away from the feared other as the source of danger and destruction. This feared other can be someone out there in the world, or someone who occupies a place within our own heart (such as a feared parent or sibling). We erect walls because a part of our self believes they will protect and save us. A social wall might be constructed of concrete and steel, whereas an interior wall might be the so-called thick skin we develop around our heart, distancing us from our true feelings and longings. Just as with tall border walls between nations, the barriers within the soul cast long, dark shadows, dispelling the living daylight of truth. If we cannot receive and feel, we cannot understand, which means we cannot grow and mature in Christ heart.

A seemingly well-known biblical story is perhaps an unlikely source of fresh guidance. Familiar tales, such as the baptism of Jesus narrated in the opening verses of the Marcan community's Gospel, tend to foster a fogging of consciousness. We may have heard the words so many times there seems to be little, if any, poignancy left. What possible meaning could an encounter of two Jewish men in Israel have for those of us involved on the spiritual journey today, where fear constructs walls casting long shadows? The key lies in our realization that fear-based separation is the blindness that taunts and haunts and seduces the human heart. As we acknowledge our fear, develop the capacity to hold it without acting upon it, and then explore and understand and own what drives us to survive, then the dawning of Christ consciousness arises, as in the soul of Jesus. Christ consciousness is simply another way of talking about the emergence of Christ heart.

SEPARATION

We need to acknowledge that we know very little about the early years of Jesus. But archeological and textual studies, among many other disciplines, are making it possible to develop reasonable theories. The work of biblical author Bruce Chilton[1] is representative. If I understand Chilton correctly, Jesus is not a typical Jew. This is because his paternity would have been in question: Mary is an unwed mother who has been intimate with Joseph—a legendary figure of whom we know nothing. Sexual intimacy outside of marriage is not necessarily scandalous in first-century Judaism but being with child without clear knowledge of who the father is threatens blood lines and the purity of the tribe. Ignorance births fear. Such a child would have been categorized as a *mamzer* and removed from typical or customary forms of religious socialization, such as gathering with the other boys and men for religious instruction. In keeping with the regulations laid down in Leviticus, fear for religious purity—and the status it was believed to have

1. See Chilton, *Rabbi Jesus*.

secured in society and before Adonai—would have led to the separation of the tainted child. Fear motivated the withdrawal from the company of the perceived impure Jesus.

Some scholars also propose that Jesus, at some point in his early teen years, very well could have made his way to the Essenes at Qumran, where he would have come to know another somewhat legendary and enigmatic figure, John the Baptist. The Essenes were Jewish ascetics. When they surveyed early first-century Jewish culture, they perceived collusion and compromise of the faith at all the critical fulcrums: the priestly Sadducees ran temple worship through cooperation with the Roman authorities; Jewish daily life was a series of compromises with Greco-Roman culture; Jewish faith was rapidly deteriorating with the chosen people living less and less like serious adherents of the covenant. Survival depended upon separation and the hills were their walls behind which they withdrew for survival.

Jesus was thus a marginal Jew—which is to say someone on the edges of dominant cultural life. He also likely came to find himself in the company of men who had chosen to be marginalized due to the spiritual corruption of the very people who had judged Jesus to be impure. (The ironies of fear-based separation never cease to abound; walls beget more walls.)

And so, the Essenes moved themselves away from quotidian Jewish life and congregated in the hills of Qumran. Here they purified themselves through ritual baths (or baptisms). Here they ate little and wore little, exposing themselves to the harsh elements to tame the beastly sexual and social instincts. This was a community for men only, thereby lessening the possibility of contamination and temptation. The end days were coming that would usher in the final battle, and if they were to be ready, separation from all distraction and purification of the wandering and desiring heart was absolutely necessary.

The souls of John and Jesus imbibed this Essene ascetical spirituality, perhaps for several years—fear-driven withdrawal in the hope of salvation through separation.

WATERS OF SEPARATION OR UNION?

We don't know exactly when, but at some point both John and Jesus departed Qumran. John, however, seems to have only left the community in a geographic sense. If the biblical accounts are to be believed, he continued life as an ascetic—he ate and wore little, and he preached his baptism of repentance. John was not only *not of* the world, but we might also say he was barely *in* the world. And for good reason, for according to his heart the world was a place of temptation and corruption. Essene spirituality still shaped his soul. He perceived the river Jordan as waters separating pure from impure. He proclaimed a baptism of repentance for the forgiveness of sins. And the sin had to do with continued collusion and cooperation with the wayward world. Sin, in other words, was failure to remain separate.[2]

Only because of what is to ensue can we say that Jesus's decision to receive John's baptism of repentance is rather a stunning awakening. Contrary to the dominant teaching of Christianity, Jesus clearly accepts John's invitation to understand himself as a sinner with the need to repent of his sin and enter the waters of the Jordan. But, as I understand it, Jesus repents of a very different sin than that governing the religious imagination of John. John understands sin as failure to remain separate. Jesus's heart, by contrast, knows sin as the false understanding of ourselves as separate, not only from God but from one another and even from our own true heart. From within the womb of Judaism, Jesus inverts the spirituality of John and births a new perspective—a spiritual path of union; a path generated from trust, not driven by fear. This is the birthing of Christ heart.

DAWNING OF CHRIST CONSCIOUSNESS

Along the way of leaving Qumran and receiving baptism from John, Jesus begins to realize that he and his Abba (Holy Mystery) are not separate. He begins to experience that there is nothing of impurity distancing his being from Adonai. He is the Beloved of Abba. This dawning realization of his true nature will come to fruition in the spirituality of John's Gospel: "The Father and I are one" (John 10:30). This is the spiritual core of the Johannine community—Jesus and Holy Mystery are One and infinitely intimate. But this intimacy is in no sense exclusive, which is where Christianity has often gone astray. Each of us is the Beloved. That is the revelatory crux of

---

2. When Israel was in Babylonian captivity, separation was essential to Jewish survival. The Babylonians practiced an ancient form of what today we might well describe as ethnic cleansing. Jewish self-preservation depended in large part on the capacity to resist Babylonian assimilation by developing and adhering to new tribal laws (such as circumcision and dietary prescriptions) that maintained a separate Jewish identity. With time, however, circumstances and contexts change. A new spiritual perspective responsive to new realities, and capable of embracing the past while simultaneously transcending its limitations, is needed. Such a perspective arises with Jesus.

Dawning of Christ Consciousness

Jesus's realization spoken of so powerfully in the Gospel of Thomas. The author of this Gospel understands that each of us is to realize the same truth as Jesus, and thereby be a Christ twin (the meaning of the Greek *didymus*, or Thomas) in Christ consciousness. "Lift the stone, you will find me there. Split the piece of wood, I am there" (Gos. Thom. 77:2–3 *NNT*). There is no creature (including a piece of wood) in which the reality of Holy Mystery is not present as its being.[3] Spirit animates all that is.

We are much nearer the truth when we recognize that sin, or better said, blindness, is failing to realize that union is the truth of the human condition. Not only the human condition, but the condition of creation. Holy Mystery is the Source and essential nature of all that is. And more, boundless love is the fabric of our true nature. The real potential that is love is the power of Spirit.

We can describe the rest of Jesus's life as the gradual discovery of what it is to be a human being who lives from the truth that Love is his Reality. He is the Beloved of the Beloved, as are we, and his life is one of boundless devotion to Holy Mystery. The baptism of Jesus is a story of the dawning of Christ consciousness: a heart awakening to the truth that all of reality is always already One. Not One in a numerical sense, but One as being a unified whole without boundaries. Like Jesus, we are on the spiritual path of realizing how to live a life with this truth as its core: a life of emerging Christ consciousness.

---

3. Three wonderful resources for the spiritual journey: Douglas-Klotz, *Revelations of the Aramaic Jesus*; Taussig, *New New Testament*; Pagels, *Beyond Belief.*

PART TWO: UNFOLDING

EXPLORATIONS

1. What are the walls fear moves you to build to preserve your safety?
2. How does fear move you to withdraw from yourself, from others?
3. What are the fear-stories that continue to shape your soul?
4. What is the impact on your soul to realize that sin is a mistaken perception of separation from others and Holy Mystery.
5. How do you not experience love as your essence?
6. How do you experience love as your essence?

Reflection 6

Becoming the Fullness of What We Already Are

Don't turn to another beggar,
You belong exclusively to Us.
Don't sell yourself short, you are priceless.

"You Yourself Are the Melody," in *Love's Ripening: Rumi on the Heart's Journey*

THROUGHOUT HIS POIGNANT AND moving book *In the Realm of Hungry Ghosts*, the Vancouver physician Gabor Maté offers heartrending accounts of the existential devastation wrought on the fabric of our personal being by the effects of addiction. One particularly graphic description strikes at the core of the human struggle.

> "The reason I do drugs is so I don't feel the fucking feelings I feel when I don't do drugs," Nick, a forty-year-old heroin and crystal meth addict once told me, weeping as he spoke. "When I don't feel the drugs in me, I get depressed." His father drilled into his twin sons the notion that they were nothing but "pieces of shit."

Nick's brother committed suicide as a teenager; Nick became a lifelong addict.[1]

Lest we facilely remove addiction from our life by reducing it ever so narrowly to the craving for drugs, Maté advises us to reassess our prejudice. Addiction, in some form or another, may well affect most of us. This gifted physician of body and soul astutely observes that "there are people who are not addicts in the strict sense, but only because their carefully constructed 'personality' works well enough to keep them from the painful awareness of their emptiness."[2]

We each often crave something to keep us from feeling, sensing, being with the immediate truth of who we are. Not all that different from Nick, we defend from knowing a truth about ourself that we believe would be unbearable. We can and often do fear what we feel the truth about our true nature might really be: an intrinsic hole of deficiency.[3] We simply don't measure up. As a result, differing only in degree from Nick, we experience a rending of the fabric of our self, and so we feel cut off from Being itself, from Holy Mystery. We feel less than the whole we actually are.

Let me frame this existential struggle in terms of the spiritual path of Rabbi Jesus, distinguishing two dimensions of the human journey: his realization of the truth of his being, and the slow process of becoming the fullness of this truth. What we are exploring is how Jesus exemplifies the spiritual journey as both discovery and development: as human beings we exist both to discover the eternal truth of what we are as boundless love as well as to develop through experience this love into the fullness of who we are in our historical lives.

DISCOVERY (REALIZATION)

The various Gospel stories of Jesus's baptism by John in the river Jordan (Mark 1:9–10, Matt 3:16–17, Luke 3:2–22) are spiritual accounts of awakening, similar to stories we find in East and West. After perhaps years of

---

1. Maté, *Realm of Hungry Ghosts*, 14.

2. Maté, *Realm of Hungry Ghosts*, 419.

3. As a student of the Diamond Approach for the past seventeen years, I draw continually from the wisdom of A. H. Almaas, its cofounder, as well as my home Diamond Group. For a fuller exploration of the human experience of holes of deficiency see Almaas, *Elements of the Real in Man*. I agree, however, with the critique of Ken Wilber that Almaas's work would benefit from an integration of "postmodern currents." See Wilber, *Integral Spirituality*, 285.

ascetical formation at the hands of the Essenes at Qumran, Jesus receives a baptism of renunciation in the ancient demarcating waters of Israel. And yet, contrary to all expectations, Jesus does not continue a ministry in the dualistic ascetic vein of the Essenes and John. Even though John preached a harrowingly prophetic winnowing word of divine judgment, Jesus experiences the true nature of his own heart as one of belovedness—"You are my dearly loved child, in whom I delight," sings his soul (Mark 1:11 *NNT*).

The dominating *external* gaze of John's judgment, which had located the source of suffering in the other and so sought to winnow away the Pharisees and Sadducees, is unexpectedly replaced by an unwavering *internal* gaze beholding human beauty as it simply is. This is a profound shift in spiritual perspective. Whereas John beholds the other as the basic problem, Jesus feels drawn into the internal desert to discover and understand where and why his own heart continues to resist love (the biblical temptations in the desert). The winnowing that will indeed occur in Jesus's own life will be that of his own self. In contrast to the experience of Nick in Maté's account, for Rabbi Jesus this will not be a hot winnowing of shaming judgment, but a refreshing cool breeze revealing the original beauty that has lain fallow for far too long.

What the biblical stories seek to convey in the mythically brief episodes of baptism is Jesus's seemingly sudden realization of the truth of his nature as a human being; the claustrophobic ghetto of fear and judgment gives way to what feels like heavenly azure expanse as he experiences the fabric of his self as one of belovedness. The scene is a vivid and striking portrayal. My sense is that the depiction of suddenness is deceiving. Jesus's new spiritual perspective is the fruit of a slow birthing process.

We know so little about the early years of Jesus, and the theory of his time with the Essenes—although with merit—is a hypothesis. Whatever the ins and outs of his early youth and teen years, he remains able and willing to feel what he feels. He is beyond the existential prison in which Nick finds himself. He has not felt himself completely cut off from the depth of his being. Even when confronted by the charismatic presence and powerful preaching of the John figure, his own experience of baptism—his experience of Holy Mystery as the pulse of his heart—is one of love and even joyful delight. But even more, it is an experience of love that is germinal; the love will grow—becoming Christ heart—if Jesus accepts the invitation to explore and understand the encounters life will throw his way.

In other words, Rabbi Jesus has a chance to become his Christic truth—one who realizes that the human life he lives is one always already graced as a gift from Holy Mystery.

DEVELOPMENT (BECOMING)

When we say that Jesus has a chance to become Christ, we're saying he, like each one of us, is offered the possibility of discovering the truth the Bible describes poetically as "finding one pearl of great value" (see Matt 13:45–46). The reference to a great price conveys the reality that personal discovery and maturation comes at a cost. Will Nick discover the courageous capacity to feel what he feels? A willingness to feel into, sense into, explore into, the nature of the heart, is the existential nature of courage. Is Jesus's deepest desire to be fed, whatever the cost? To be comfortable, whatever the cost? To be in control of life, whatever the cost? These are the (desert) temptations to avoid feeling the fullness of being a human being. The willingness to explore the life we have before us, the biblical wilderness, is the unfolding journey of becoming the fullness of our true nature. Jesus grows into his personal Christ-ness as he more fully embodies the boundless love he experienced himself to be at his baptism. He experiences, explores, and comes to understand the truth of the hungers of his fearful desire to control. He is becoming, he is being birthed as, a Christ heart.

But it is also true that he is not becoming something he is not already by nature. This misperception of a gap has haunted and distorted the dominant form of Christian spirituality. Holy Mystery *is* boundless love. Being *is* boundless love: this is the experience of Jesus described so beautifully in the poetic Gospel stories of baptism. Holy Mystery is not circumscribed but Reality itself. Love is not a *choice* of Holy Mystery but the true nature of Mystery itself, which is why we call Mystery *Holy*. What this means is that we are awakening to the truth that it is an impossibility—that is, it simply could not ever be—that Jesus, or any creature, be anything but a manifestation of Boundless Love. We can, very often do, act to restrict and cordon off love. But this boundless love, without edges or shores, is the real potential that is the great pearl, realized at great price.

Jesus, in his nature or on his journey, is not essentially different from any other person, nor could he be, because Holy Mystery is the true nature of all creatures. His life and journey are a living invitation (and testament) to also become who we already are. Jesus is Christ inviting all to discover

Becoming the Fullness of What We Already Are

their own Christ-ness. Each creature, like Jesus, is an utterly unique embodiment of Holy Mystery, a pearly potential of love.

We are so often blind to our true nature, yet do not know it. In our blindness we are terrified, just like Nick. Our own convictions feel all too real, but they are false. False in that they are the contours of a perspective that imprisons us, by holding us back from feeling, sensing, exploring what is truly in our heart; what is truly our heart. Our pearly potential rubs up against these limiting walls that are not wrong but deceiving. We discover the deception through the grit of the daily rub, which is Being inviting us to explore and wonder. Maté, following the wise lead of teacher A. H. Almaas, reminds us that the person of addiction must be willing to enter with wonderment if they are to know the healing of the hole of fear in their heart. This spiritual truth obtains for us all—we come to know the truth of who we are only if we are willing to enter and explore. Yet—and here is the authentically merciful quality of Holiness of Mystery—regardless, the truth of our real potential abides in us and as us. Although we may feel lost to life, life is never lost to us because love is the heart of Reality itself.

Julian of Norwich proclaimed, in the face of an oppressive and dominant atonement spirituality of human depravity, that "all will be well."[4] Julian knew she was expressing a bold vision of universalism (i.e., no one could ever be lost to Love), flying in the face of Christianity that taught its people to expressly not feel, not sense, not explore the stirrings of their personal heart. All will be well, but what a difference it makes when we experientially know that for ourselves. Much of Nick's soulful suffering is in the conviction of being of no worth and lost to life; he fears this is his true truth, full stop.

Almaas reminds us what generations of mystics have taught: "the universe is a theophany, and its changes are the life of God."[5] Nothing could

---

4. Julian, *Showings*, 225.

5. See Almaas, *Facets of Unity*, 57–58. Although Almaas reminds us of the theological insight of mystics and theologians past, I differ from the conclusion he draws about the nature of God in the West as a "projection"; sometimes a projection, but not always. My understanding is closer to that of Karl Rahner expressed in *Foundations*, where he understands "nature" to be a *Restbegriff*; that is, Reality as we live and know it is a unity of natural and supernatural. Nature is what would remain (i.e., a remainder concept, or *Restbegriff*) if one theoretically could strip away the supernatural (which is impossible). This is because God "communicates his own divine reality and makes it a constitutive element in the fulfillment of the creature." 121. In my words, God—Holy Mystery—is of the very reality of the human being and, I would add, of every creature and of all existence. Writes Rahner, "God's self-communication [is] a permanent existential of

PART TWO: UNFOLDING

ever cut us off from the reality of Holy Mystery because life itself, as it is in each unfolding moment, is the mystery of boundless love.[6]

The universe is a sacrament, manifesting Holy Mystery, fresh, moment to moment. There is only one boundless Reality, and it is a gracious one, as it is this dynamic manifestation of the universal Holy Mystery in its myriad beauty—and that includes the full spectrum of human suffering and loss. The invitation Reality extends to us all, just as with Rabbi Jesus, is to realize the truth of our real potential—we are boundless love waiting to mature. Our soul's deep longing is to explore this truth, developing along the journey the pearl of great price each of us is invited to be by our very gracious nature. Thereby, we may become the fullness of who we already are. Our heart is ready to blossom as Christ heart.

[human beings]."118. As we fully awaken, I would add that Holy Mystery is the Heart of our heart, the Source and Sustainer of Reality. As Source, all that is is flowing forth as expression of Holy Mystery—not to be misunderstood as a circumscribed "self" but as communication of infinite Deep, moment to moment.

6. St. Paul, in his letter to the community at Rome, captures this awareness when he writes: "For I am persuaded that neither death, nor life, nor angels, nor archangels, nor the present, nor the future, nor any powers, nor height, nor depth, nor any other created thing, will be able to separate us from the love of God revealed in Christ Jesus, our Lord!" (Rom 8:38–39 *NNT*).

EXPLORATIONS

1. What are some of the ways you feel less than whole? What feels right to you about feeling less than whole?

2. As you feel your heart now and sense your body, what arises as your sense of the truth of what you are in this moment? What experiences are central to your sense of self?

3. As you gaze within, what ways do you discover your heart resists love?

4. What are some of the ways you feel the fullness of being a human being? What stops you from feeling your fullness?

5. Love is not a choice of Holy Mystery. Love is the true nature of Holy Mystery. How does this truth impact your heart in this moment?

6. In what ways are you discovering your own heart as Holy Mystery? Your own being as Christ heart?

7. What holds you back from turning within to explore your Christ heart?

Reflection 7

Living Christs of Touch

In the beginning the Word was;
and the Word was with God;
and the Word was God.
The Word was in the beginning with God;
through the Word all things came into being
and nothing came into being apart from the Word.

JOHN 1:1–3 *NNT*

And the Word became flesh,
and lived among us.

JOHN 1:14 *NNT*

IF YOU WERE IN hospice care because your life was ending and you were given the chance to write a few words to encapsulate its essence, what would you say? The story wouldn't have to be historical, or literally true, but it would need to offer an authentic window into your soul and the heart of your heart.

I find it fruitful to read John's Gospel from this perspective. I am amazed with the story John writes for us as offering the essence of Rabbi

Jesus. This is the only Gospel in which, as Jesus's death approaches, he is depicted as caring for his friends by touching their bodies—no meal, a few words, and the washing of feet. Of all the possible stories John could have created to convey the heart of Jesus's life—a stunning miracle or a captivating oration—the Gospel author simply presents Jesus as essentially engaging in tender and intimate touch. Inviting his friends to do the same (which is so much more than learning to imitate).

As his prospect for survival fades and the death of his bodily self approaches, Jesus does not retreat, nor does he attack, nor is he frozen with fear. He surprisingly reaches out. He loves—not abstractly, not theoretically. Jesus teaches his spiritual path through embodiment. The depth of his own realization manifests in the utter simplicity of his action. His Christic heart loves, even in the face of Roman crucifixion. In Jesus, the human survival instinct, where we are driven at almost all costs to preserve our bodily self, is not destroyed. The instinct is transformed as it is subsumed into a larger seamless Reality—within John's brief account we are offered a vision of a spiritual path for humanity that is one of a revolutionary mystic.

I continue to ponder Yuval Noah Harari's insightful and provocative book *Sapiens: A Brief History of Humankind*. Harari pierces the bubble of the pervasive myth that *Homo sapiens* reign triumphant at the summit of evolution after a rather peaceful, solitary, and linear development. On the contrary, he chronicles how the dawn of *Homo sapiens* is marred by our genocide of at least two other human species with whom we shared this earth—Denisovans and Neanderthals. Initially retreating to East Africa after feeling their survival threatened, our ancient forebears reemerged, attacked, and destroyed. Although there was some interbreeding among the various human species, detectable today in our own DNA, this was minimal. But not only did our ancestors annihilate other humans, they were then responsible for the decimation of the majority of large mammals in Australia and the Americas (once thought to have been due to precipitous climate change).

This violent dawn of the history of *Homo sapiens* was a harbinger of countless tragedies to come over the following millennia. Often religion, as a cultural force that binds groups together, reinforced and offered justification for the destruction of others whose presence was perceived as threatening one's own, and one's tribe's, survival. Touch was neither tender nor intimate—it was terrifyingly terminal.

Harari's book is a sobering testament: Our species kills, and we destroy the lives of others readily and easily. When we fear for the survival of our bodily self we sometimes freeze up, but rather more often we feel compelled to retreat to find safety or we ruthlessly attack; think of the Rwandan genocide of 1994 or the more recent Russian invasion of Ukraine. Our nervous system feels overwhelmed, and we react out of desperation.

Apart from Harari's historical perspective, what I'm describing is not new. But the information does highlight the significance of John's story about Jesus. Jesus is a wisdom figure in that vein of Axial[1] spiritual teachers (chronicled in such illustrative detail by Karen Armstrong in *The Great Transformation*) who has realized that another human path is not only possible, such a path is absolutely necessary. Otherwise, our species will likely not survive, and neither will so many of the other magnificent and irreplaceable creatures with whom we share this sphere.

John's story of Jesus is the genesis of a new kind of spiritual path arising in Judaism—a revolutionary mystical path that offers *Homo sapiens* a chance for our survival instinct not to be destroyed (which is impossible), but to be transformed by being incorporated into a larger Reality (John 17:21, "that all may be one").

If this path is to be fruitful, then Christianity will need to discover how to form faith communities that are sources of instinctual transformation rather than belief clubs that reinforce the fear and prejudice and destruction deeply rooted in our species. This is complex, and our focus is simply one questioning thread within evolution's tapestry: Why do we exist as a Christian community? Even more fundamentally, what is it that is utterly unique about spiritual communities? What do we have to offer humanity that is absolutely necessary? The answer, as far as I can tell, has to do with realizing that our love of life needs to mature into the love of Holy Mystery, which includes, yet transcends, the love of our bodily self.

---

1. Another excellent study of the Axial Age is found in Bellah, *Religion in Human Evolution*. A good summary of the Axial Age is found in the *Encyclopedia Britannica*: "The Axial Age (also called Axis Age) is the period when, roughly at the same time around most of the inhabited world, the great intellectual, philosophical, and religious systems that came to shape subsequent human society and culture emerged—with the ancient Greek philosophers, Indian metaphysicians and logicians (who articulated the great traditions of Hinduism, Buddhism, and Jainism), Persian Zoroastrianism, the Hebrew Prophets, the 'Hundred Schools' (most notably Confucianism and Daoism) of ancient China. . . . These are only some of the representative Axial traditions that emerged and took root during that time. The phrase originated with the German psychiatrist and philosopher Karl Jaspers, who noted that during this period there was a shift—or a turn, as if on an axis—away from more predominantly localized concerns and toward *transcendence*." Stefon, "Axial Age," para. 2.

I believe that the one gift that a spiritual community can offer that is utterly unique is that of being an experiential school providing an effective path for a soul to realize her true nature as a manifestation of Holy Mystery, and then serve creation as best we can. My sense is that this describes John's community (as well as that of Thomas). John's Gospel has its own language to express this realization—Jesus comes to know himself as the Word become flesh. In John's experience, when Holy Mystery speaks, the Logos manifests, and in history Jesus comes to be as the Logos. (Remember, this is poetry, not literal prose.)

As we unpack the poetic insight of John, the Deep resounds and the song that is life sings. Each creature is a note of the Deep's voice. There is no gap between the Deep and the singing. Breath is expressed in sound and sound is shaped as word. Creatures are the sounding Words of Holy Mystery. A spirituality of Being is a radical and revolutionary mysticism in which all gaps disappear.

Radical means rooted. Each and every creature is rooted in and as Holy Mystery. We are each words uniquely shaping the exhalation (the creating flowing forth) as Being. This means that spiritual communities exist essentially that we might realize this truth of our nature and in this realization become enraptured with the song of creating. Spiritual communities exist to invite us to fall in love with the moist breath of Reality arising from our own depths—a Deep Source that never dies.

In his captivating book *Resurrecting Jesus: Embodying the Spirit of a Revolutionary Mystic*, Adyashanti writes in the spirit of John. He recognizes that "religion's primary function is not about conveying ethical and moral codes; it is not about politics and power and hierarchy. Religion's primary function is to awaken within us the experience of the sublime and to connect us with the mystery of existence. As soon as religion forgets about its roots in the eternal, it fails in its central task."[2]

I would modify Adyashanti's primary function of religion (I prefer to speak of spirituality). The common ground and common good are integrally related (as we discussed above in reflection 3). This means that the soul's awakening cannot help but include our love of and care for the society and culture in which we live. As Holy Mystery, love through and through, we awaken *and* serve. Service is not driven by fear or command but is the heart's divine desire to restore justice where there is suffering. Awakening and service are two dimensions of one Reality (a truth long recognized in

---

2 Adyashanti, *Resurrecting Jesus*, 23.

the wisdom of addiction healing/recovery). Adyashanti's admonition is correct, however, in that as soon as religion/spirituality forgets the dimension of awakening, with that failing we are reduced to bestial destruction. Spirituality becomes a hollow shell of strident moral righteousness justifying our fears and desires to perpetuate the existence of our bodily self at all costs.

If we, as *Homo sapiens*, do not awaken to the sublime and realize our connection with Holy Mystery, we will not know how to touch each other and the creatures of creation, tenderly. Without our connection with Holy Mystery, we will continue our history of the destruction of life. But—with our realization that the mystery of Spirit is our true nature, then it becomes possible for us to mature, like Jesus, into revolutionary mystics. We become no longer preoccupied with the defensive protection of our small bodily self. We develop the capacity to be open to touch and healing in the face of threat. We are Christ heart. We become, not imitators of Jesus, but living, creative Christs, where Word touches Word, and bodily death is incapable of harming or destroying our Reality.

EXPLORATIONS

1. What were your earliest experiences of touch? Were they tender, respectful, appropriately intimate and nourishing? Or were they intrusive, invasive? Were they traumatic? (By traumatic, I mean anything that exceeded your capacity at the time to defend against.)

2. How would you describe your spiritual community, if you have one? Is it a belief club with firm doctrine and hard boundaries? If so, how does that impact the capacity of your heart and body to relax and receive? Is it an experience-based school respectful of your integrity and journey to realize your true nature as an expression of Holy Mystery? If so, how does that impact the capacity of your heart and body to relax and receive?

3. In what ways do you experience yourself as a note, a song, of the Deep's voice? What does your note or song sound like? Find a place to speak or sing your note or song. How does it resonate in your heart and your body and your mind? How would you describe your experience? Enjoyable, anxious, unsure?

4. What are some of the ways your soul withdraws or closes from a sense of fear? What are some of the ways you experience your soul open to touch and healing in the face of hatred?

Reflection 8

The Courage to See

There is no such thing as doing right or wrong when there is freedom.
You *are* free and from that centre you act.
And hence there is no fear, and a mind that has no fear is capable of great love.
And when there is love it can do what it will.

Krishnamurti, *Freedom from the Known*

It is an existential conundrum for us human beings that we long for someone to see us for the truth of what we are, while at the same time fearing to be seen for the truth of what we *think* we are and that others might perceive. A very tiring dance.

There is the all-too-resonant story told in 2 Kings of the Hebrew Scriptures about an army commander, Naaman, who is suffering from a skin disease the author describes with the ancient catchall *leprosy*. He is, we are told, a great man held in high favor. But he is plagued by this disease that is so deplorable in large part because it is visible to all. Naaman travels to the entrance of the prophet Elisha's house with the hope of being cured. The prophet sends him a messenger with instructions for cleansing.

But Naaman becomes incensed and angry, turning away in a rage. The aggravating issue for Naaman is that Elisha doesn't seem to know who he is dealing with. Can't he recognize Naaman's greatness, which is there for all to acknowledge if they simply look? But why feel enraged about being overlooked? Because the issue is the tissue of a deep and searing wound, which even if not visible, festers and enslaves this supposedly great man.

There is more than a bit of Naaman in all of us. His condition is our own. We bear a mostly unconscious wound that twists our soul in knots of fear and confuses the longing of our heart, and often we erupt in anger or even rage when we are not taken as the image we project and hold so dear. Yet, we are also terrified of being seen for our truth. As I said, a very tiring dance, and it begins when we are very young.

BLISS AND WOUND

To behold a mother cradling her newborn infant as her own heart regulates and settles the breathing of the child, as the two merge into one field of graceful relaxation that is warm and expansive and at complete ease—this union is a wonder of life. A newborn knows her mother's voice amidst the cacophony of sounds rushing upon her infant ears. Very soon after, this little one's eyes recognize the countenance of her mom. The mother's and infant's eyes behold each other in a river of love that eases into a graceful lake of which both are simply two peaceful waves.

I believe in this experience lies much of the origin of what Christianity calls *the beatific vision*—our direct encounter with the beauty that is Holy Mystery. The divine is self-expressing as two beautiful beings beholding one another: Deep unto Deep. The bliss is boundless. The child's body completely relaxes, expanding as a sweet, pink essence as her soul is seen as its true nature: she is nothing but Holy Mystery being embodied here and now. The soul's deep longing is satisfied, and this complete satisfaction saturates this tiny being. The soul has been kissed from within by her deepest truth and intuitively knows it.

Because the bliss is completely, soulfully satisfying, its loss is a searing wound. Sometimes the loss comes at once as a traumatic rupture, but oftentimes it accrues slowly as the sensitive touch of Holy Mystery upon the soul diminishes to a memory (a memory both alluring and haunting). The toddler between nine and fourteen months, with the newly discovered capacity to first crawl and then walk, begins to separate and become an individual on an adventure. The infant's life, once restricted to a relatively black-and-white spectrum of ankles and shins and table legs, explodes into the toddler's technicolor panorama of life's infinite expressions.

OUR CONUNDRUM

She steps out. She stops. She turns. Does mom see what an incredible thing is happening? Does mom see *her*? She does. The toddler is beside herself with joy. Mom is beholding her magnificence—not only what she is doing but who she is as the one that is doing it. Her being registers the mother's beholding as a soulful seeing. But then, there inevitably are the times when she turns, and mom does *not* see her. Mom is looking, but not appreciatively present. Mom is elsewhere (and there is no one to blame). Perhaps she is preoccupied with last night, or with tomorrow, or with tensions with her partner. Maybe simply exhausted. And so, the little toddler unconsciously wonders, what must I do to get her to see me?

This little child becomes someone who learns to perform so that mom will look her way. What surface activity will draw mom's attention? We learn to act, regardless of how we feel, in such a way that mom, or dad, or whoever the important other is, will notice us, our greatness, our uniqueness, our beauty. But the trap for the soul has been laid—the action no longer reflects who we are, but who we believe we need to be for someone else to look our way and affirm our value. And we come to believe that we are valued not for who we are, but for how we perform—how we appear. In fact, we become unconsciously terrified that who we are is not valuable enough, not beautiful enough, to be seen. We become afraid of being seen for what we believe is our true nature—something woefully deficient and unworthy of being beheld. We long and we fear what we long for.

This loss of contact with our own self is sometimes described as a narcissistic wound.[1] We lose contact with the true potential of who we are, and the result is a wounding hole in our soul which is unbearable. What has happened is that we have lost our sense of self, so we hunger for sources to tell us who and what we are (which is the narcissism). We bandage over the original wound, unhealed, with strips of various identities we take on; identities that have garnered us the attention, the approval, the admiration, of others. The looks of others provide us with an endless supply of bandages.

---

1. See Almaas, *Point of Existence*, 217–18. For Almaas, narcissism is the result of the soul's identification with anything other than her true nature.

But the wound remains, and it festers without the air of truth to heal it. We continue to hunger to be seen as someone.[2]

Every so often something pushes up hard against it and the pain can be both searing and crushing. We angrily demand to be looked upon and appreciated for all our accomplishments, for they reassure us of our wobbly worth. Like Naaman, we can explode with such hot rage because we are so hurt. The wound runs deep within and way back to our childhood. What we are longing for, in part, is for someone to see us for the truth—the love—of who we are; to show us a way to recover and realize our soul's vitality; to see through the false bravado of bandages; to behold our beauty undetermined by any accomplishment and untarnished by any failure; to behold us for our beautiful, pearly potential. And yet, we are terrified to be seen so naked and vulnerable.

FAITH: THE COURAGE TO SEE

Such is the gift Luke's Jesus offers the lepers in his story of chapter 17. Whereas Naaman's bandaged persona has enabled him to be looked upon as a great man, these lepers are people stripped bare even of names. They are looked upon as a blatantly raw category. They are a disease that causes dis-ease in the community. No beauty. No value. Eyes look upon the surface only, in order *not* to see. Their presentation appears both dismal and abhorrent to the onlooker. Surprisingly perhaps, unlike with Naaman, the story speaks of no anger or rage in these nameless ones. That is because the soulful collapse of these homeless beings is almost total. They have no land, no place, no people. Their infinite, soulful depth has been crushed to a scarred dermal surface. They believe that the story about who they are is true. They feel they are nothing.

Until Jesus, the story goes, *saw* them. Like wobbly toddlers, these human beings take tentative steps, look up and—Jesus does not look at them. He sees into them. *He beholds their beauty.* Beauty of the same divine Being as his own, which is why he can see them. There is no gap; no distance. They are of the one Deep and his seeing is an invitation to their souls to awaken to this inherent truth. His gaze is a direct and tender and strong beholding. His seeing is the Christic heart of perception born of the realization of his own unsurpassable beauty as an expression of Holy Mystery.

---

2. One way of appreciating the nine types of the Enneagram is as various identities the self takes on to cover up its sense of absence, or its experience of a hole.

Part Two: Unfolding

To awaken is neither easy nor for the faint of heart. We have lived with our anger, our rage, our collapse, for decades—they are the devils we at least know. The bandages may be old and ineffective, but we are used to them, and they've come to feel like part of us. And so it is in the story; for only one of these human beings does the gaze of Jesus land upon the soul as the Christic kiss of peace. This person, too, begins to see, to behold, their own beauty. There is no performance here to capture a glance. No need to look a certain way in order to receive love. The seeing is the initial realization of self-worth and self-beauty, of authentic self-hood. This is a gracious beginning made possible because Jesus saw them. He beholds their heart with his heart—a single Christic heart.

Luke's story ends with Jesus saying, "Your faith has made you well" (Luke 17:19), which means the courage for us to see into our own soul and discover its inherent and integral and unsurpassable beauty is wholeness making. This is the path of realizing Christ heart. Faith here is the willingness to trust what we experience, no longer trapped by our concern about what others think or judge us to be, no longer imprisoned by our concern about what we have thought ourselves to be in the past. We move beyond looking, a move made possible because another was present and capable of seeing us as our true nature, regardless of our performance. And we begin to trust what our Christic soul sees, and she sees unsurpassable beauty as her truth.

EXPLORATIONS

1. Describe your earliest memories of being held, of being seen, by your primary caregiver. What feelings arise in your heart and what sensations surface in your body?

2. We become little doers at a very young age, developing our capacity to secure attention and love. How did you act or perform as a child to gain your primary caregiver's approving gaze? (Be a helper, get things right, get out of the way, achieve, be entertaining, etc.)

3. How have you bandaged over your wounds of not being beheld as beautiful just as you are, not for what you did?

4. Who has truly seen you for who you are? How has their seeing helped you to turn within and behold your own beauty and innate goodness?

5. Identify the ways you see yourself for who you truly are.

6. One way to describe faith is as the willingness to trust what you experience. Explore the ways you doubt your experience and the ways you trust your experience.

Reflection 9

Holy Wisdom

> You have placed your truth in the inner being;
> therefore, teach me the wisdom of the heart.
> Forgive all that binds me in fear
> that I might radiate love;
> cleanse me that your light shine in me.
>
> Merrill, "Psalm 51," in *Psalms for Praying*

Wisdom is often spoken about in spirituality. What do we mean by its use? How is our spiritual practice a wise practice? How does authentic spiritual wisdom differ from conventional life of the world? We extoll wisdom in poetry, song, and art. Wisdom can be understood as "the quality of having experience, knowledge, and good judgment."[1] But what kind of experience? What kind of knowledge? What kind of judgment is good?

When we are held in our mother's womb we are fed as needed through the umbilical cord. We are kept warm as needed through our mother's thermoregulation. We float nestled in her amniotic sea, our tiny body suspended and trusting in the wise capacity to provide of fluid Holy Mystery. This

---

1. Oxford Languages, s.v. "Wisdom."

trust is kinesthetic; we are a long way from being self-conscious. We know trust as a somatic truth, as our being is inclined to trust from conception.[2]

We can see this bodily trust as we reflect on our existence as newborn infants, lying languidly in our mother's arms. We experience life for the most part as what the English psychoanalyst and pediatrician D. W. Winnicott coined as "good enough."[3] Not perfect, but good enough. Life doesn't need to be perfect for us to thrive; simply good enough. When we are hungry—mom feeds us. When our bowels are full—we relieve ourself. When tired—our tiny being slumbers. Reality simply and sufficiently provides, and our infant sense of trust is visible in our relaxed mouth and eyes; in our tranquil arms lying loose upon our undulating and soft belly. We live *with*—no, it is even more intimate—we live *as* an abiding trust in the wisdom of Holy Mystery to provide.

Good enough, however, does not mean we don't experience difficulties, even as young infants. Inevitable disruptions occur, and our trust is gradually whittled thin. We hunger and are not fed enough or not in a timely fashion. We are cold or too hot. Our tummy is upset, and no amount of holding is an effective remedy. We get a fever and ache. As we become toddlers and venture forth, sometimes when we look back for mom or dad they are not there. Or they are there but seem to be looking right through or past us. We fall. We experience betrayal and loss. Life seems anything but always wise (and perhaps we experience the holding as anything but good enough). The hurts and bruises to body and soul continue to accrue and the whittling of trust continues. There is a belligerence in our experience of life which, according to conventional belief, belies the presence of wisdom.

There is no one to blame. No one we need to fault. We are limited and conditioned creatures, you and me. There is no environment, no family unit, that holds us perfectly. Even with the best of motives, we all make mistakes, hurt, and are hurt. That is the human condition.

Take a few moments. And let yourself feel into the reality I'm describing. How is your heart? Is there tension? Tightness? Softness? Are you able to feel your heart? There are no right or wrong answers here. You are

---

2. Stern, in *Interpersonal World*, presents how the sense of self serves as the basic organizing principle of development, and the infant acquires new senses of the self during the first three years of life. The two earliest senses of self are the *emergent self* and the *core self*, both of which are integral bodily senses of self-in-relation-with-others. Trust exists and expresses in and through the infant's body—e.g., relaxed muscles, open eyes, regular breathing, which in time will become a conscious experience.

3. See Greenberg and Mitchell, *Object Relations in Psychoanalytic Theory*, 188–218.

(wisely) checking in with your body as it is. No agenda. Simply exploring. How does your belly feel? How does your breathing feel? What about your solar plexus, where all those nerves meet in the torso with exquisite sensitivity? We often are unaware that our loss of trust is first and foremost a bodily experience. (Our belly muscles tighten, our solar plexus can feel like a small rock, our breathing accelerates, our pupils dilate.) In the theory of Freud, the ego is firstly a body ego. Or in the view of Daniel Stern, our self is a bodily self. (This may seem obvious, but if there is one thing we tend to forget as we move into residence in our head, it is our body, our sensations, and our feelings.)

We live, move, and have our being as bodily creatures. It thus makes sense to recognize our soul is a "soulbody" (although for the sake of brevity I often simply speak of soul). You are *embodied* Spirit and the truest barometer of your state in this moment is always your body because the body does not lie or deceive. It often takes a while to fully sense into our body, which is fine. Wisdom invites compassionate curiosity. What is your sacred body revealing in this moment?

Inevitably there is a relentless thinning of trust, which takes its toll upon our soulbody. We become convinced that our survival depends upon the mind taking charge. A very specific delusion arises: since Reality seems all too unreliable, we will undertake the responsibility for directing the unfolding of our self. Our breathing quickens as body and belly contract and harden. Our brow furrows as mind kicks into overdrive. Our pace of life shifts into higher gear. Limbs tighten and withdraw. Life is no longer a mystery we receive, but a problem we must solve to survive. Contraction becomes our unconscious way of life. It's as if life has the wisdom squeezed out of it. Again, not because we are doing anything wrong. We are afraid, doubtful, and trying as hard as we can to be in charge so life won't unravel.

I am describing us as developing a sense of self that comes to mistrust Reality. Reality ceases to be Holy Mystery. Reality is more a riddle to be rightly answered, a puzzle to be correctly solved, a challenge to be overcome, and a threat to be thwarted. Our sense of self begins to live from a perspective in which Reality is power we defend against by developing skills to subdue and conquer, or endure.

We take it as common sense, the wisdom of the world, to understand ourself as a small and unsafe object separate from and at the mercy of an arbitrary or even capricious external force. By the time we are a self-consciously aware person, we simply take as common sense this perceptive framework. Only a fool would trust, and we will not be fooled. And yet, we don't know what work we *ought* to be about in order to surely and certainly direct our soul's unfolding. Which path is the correct one? Do we turn left or right? Do we go forward or backward? Do we fight or flee? There is a desperate quality to the mind's frantic search for the correct path, believing all the while that there is such a path.

One common way of reacting to the loss of trust in Reality is to step into the perceived breach and become selves who plan—constantly. Within the delusion that we, as human beings, must direct and control our soul's unfoldment, Wisdom devolves into wisdom-as-planning. Fundamental trust remains but as a foggy, somatic memory, and so we turn to the machinations of our own mind to control the vagaries of life and secure, as best we can, a course and outcome we prefer. Maybe we don't plan. Maybe we flee into our imagination. Maybe we fight, continuously. Maybe we turn to some addictive substance or lifestyle.[4]

All the reactions to survive that flow from our mistrust take enormous energy. As you feel into your heart and sense into your body, are you aware of fatigue? Weariness? Perhaps some sadness? Or heaviness? In my guidance of others, I receive people who are tired, disillusioned, angry, and often feeling defeated. Some resolve to try even harder and become like purpose-driven machines.

Kindness. Mercy. Patience. Our soulbody longs for these anointments upon our self. In my spiritual exploration classes, body movement practices, meditation sessions, and Enneagram gatherings, I offer a safe holding environment in which we may begin to relax, soften, and wonder: What does it really mean to live a wise life? To be a wise person? The wisdom of the world, which has replaced Holy Wisdom with the incessant need to do something, is experienced as less and less convincing—whatever it is we are doing. Our body knows it, even as we push to the side our contractions, ulcers, migraines, tears. Our heart and mind know it, as ceaseless mental activity leaves our heart empty and searching, our head aching. What we don't realize is that our current sense of self, in all its strategizing, is itself a limited expression of a fully authentic and mature soulful wisdom continuing to be born.

---

4. The wisdom of the Enneagram can be a helpful resource here, identifying the principal and habitual defense mechanisms, avoidances, and reactions of the different Enneagram types. Four helpful resources: Maitri, *Spiritual Dimension of the Enneagram*; Riso and Hudson, *Wisdom of the Enneagram*; Chestnut, *Complete Enneagram*; and Thew Forrester, *Holding Beauty in My Soul's Arms*.

Part Two: Unfolding

Each of us is trying so hard. I invite you to fully acknowledge and respect that about yourself. We are doing everything we can to stay above water. Our cultures give us plenty of role models who have supposedly made it by simply exerting themselves relentlessly. Within the wisdom of the world, we are here to lift ourself up. There is a paucity of truly wise elders to turn to for guidance. Too often, proffered spiritual advice is magical or moral.

I don't see such advice present in the life and teaching of the Jesus of history. In early Christianity we now know that Jesus was often understood and experienced as the embodiment of wisdom and known as Christ Sophia. *Sophia* is Greek for wisdom and *Christ* is Greek for anointed. Christ Sophia means Jesus, in realizing his own true nature, was someone who knew from experience that he was graciously woven into existence as love and this love guided his day-to-day living. As Christ Sophia, Jesus is *the* wisdom elder of the Christian spiritual tradition. He is neither a magician nor a moralist. He is a human being who has realized that boundless love is the spirit animating his life; whose life *is* a wisdom story, a birthing of Wisdom, emerging in and through the same dynamics as those I described above.

Jesus is likely the child of a young woman in a small village, whose paternity is in question and where tribal lineage remains vitally important. He is a Jewish child whose questionable status leads to being treated with suspicion, some ridicule, and perhaps a shadow of shame. A child raised in a holding environment that he could easily have experienced as dropping him on a regular basis; a child hurt and bruised and thus suspicious of the wisdom of Reality. If we move beyond the more romantic versions of biblical storytelling, here is a child that grows into an adolescent who more than likely, like all adolescents, readily questioned the tacit wisdom of Reality. In his case, a boy who matures into a young man, likely drawn to the purported certainty embodied in the apocalyptic plans of the Essenes at Qumran.

As we discovered earlier, the Essenes were disaffected Jews for whom Roman-occupied Israel was an abomination; to whom the majority of Jews had compromised their spiritual way of life in order to survive; for whom women were a temptation. The Essenes were celibate men who had fled the rest of their people to live in the hills, practicing regular ritual ablutions to cleanse themselves. They did not trust in the basic innate goodness of creation and human beings. They had become the sons of light set against the sons of darkness, preparing for the final spiritual battle of the age. It is likely that Jesus spent many months, if not a few years, with this group, searching for truth. Not yet a rabbi, he is a hurting human being initially captured by the clear, bold, and prophetic plans of John the Baptist. He is not unlike many today whose hurt leads them to a black-and-white moral world of zealotry; suffering souls searching for clarity in religious purity and moral judgment.

We are growing in wisdom as we more fully appreciate the challenge we all face. In our life, when the basic trust of the soul has faded, we feel lost. The searing absence must be filled and we do it, as best we can, with our constant planning. Remember, we begin in the womb as trusting souls, suspended in the pool of nurturing life that is our mother's womb. To lose our heartful sense of trust is to receive a wound that we cannot tolerate. We live to trust, and trusting is living.

Without a basic sense of trust in Holy Mystery, we try to direct the soul's unfolding because we don't know what else to do and feel compelled to do *something* to survive. We are afraid to relax and be, precisely because of our history of pain and suffering. Without trust we can't relax. Our body won't soften and be vulnerable. We pull back more and more into the small prison of the head with vigilant eyes. But—our heart knows there is more, which is why it aches with sorrow. Our heart continues its search. Maybe the search is muffled by addiction, by distraction, by achieving. There are so many ways we seek to assuage the heart's sorrow. Through it all, however, we long to experience true rest in the home of our soul. The true nature of our soul can never be destroyed. The ground of God and the ground of the soul, as Meister Eckhart realized, is the same ground: Holy Mystery.

The labyrinthine human journey, amazingly enough, can bring us right where we need to be. Wisdom, we are discovering, is of the spiritual fabric of life itself. Her invitation to us remains through thick and thin. The inability of taking charge to bring us rest, and the futility of constructing life out of moral judgments, are a gift. They bring our heart to the realization that the means our personality has devised for trying to survive leave us feeling both helpless and hopeless. Ordinary reactivity is not the answer for the soul. Surrender, not striving, is the soul's true path. But the striving is something we all experience and try. No judgment here.

As our striving subsides there is space for sincerity to surface in a new form—softness and tears and humility. Our soul's sincere search leads us to waters of new birth, or rebirth. Our sweat and tears are part of this healing water. The soul's question is whether Holy Mystery, washing over, in, and through us, moment to moment, is truly a womb of life in which she might trustingly rest. Only the soul can experience the answer to this question. Teachers and teachings may help. But they are only pointers.

It is no accident that the story of Jesus's adult ministry begins with the account of his initial awakening in the waters of the Jordan. These waters are the ebb and flow of life; they are the current of Reality, which we fear will overwhelm and destroy us. Jesus steps into their depths. His ascetical life at Qumran with the Essenes is over. Separation from the supposedly dark masses of humanity and ceaseless ritual ablutions have not assuaged his heart. His soulbody falls into the River Jordan, exhausted from having striven for so long. He releases his guarded heart to receive the flowing force of life full upon his soul. He allows his heart to be vulnerable. Although his person is not destroyed, the release of his planning mind, contracted heart, and defended body, begins. How? His emerging Christ heart realizes that its very substance is belovedness and that boundless love is the spiritual fabric of Reality.

We can appreciate in Rabbi Jesus's life what is true about how Wisdom invites our life to unfold. Love is the womb of trust and relaxes our constricted heart and feverishly strategizing mind. In this trust, chest and abdomen relax and soften, and brow loosens its viselike grip around our fearful eyes. We need to appreciate the vitality of the heart-mind connection. As the heart ceases to be a fortress guarded by all manner of defenses, it provides a soft, certain, and sure base upon which the mind may settle in ease. Constant planning is a heavy burden, which weighs down the soul in darkness. The rebirth of abiding trust allows the mind to lie open, allowing heavenly blue skies to suffuse the self once more. The Gospels convey this human truth in the lovely imagery of the heavens opening as Jesus realizes that he is the beloved of Holy Mystery.

Holy Wisdom is born anew in and through the womb of love. This Wisdom is not the result of planning or even more generally, doing. What is Holy about this Wisdom is that it reflects a *loving* Reality that does not work by some divine blueprint; no, Reality unfolds spontaneously, moment to moment. The practice of spirituality is learning how to participate fully in this unfoldment; no one and no thing directs it. Holy Wisdom speaks of the objective truth that each and every manifestation of Reality is an expression, an embodiment, of Holy Mystery. It is reputed that Einstein asked whether the universe is for or against us. If that remains our question, then the soul will never relax in basic trust. The more basic question for each of us is whether we realize that all that is, *is* Holy Mystery, including even us.

Holy Wisdom

What our soul longs to know is that Reality, like the womb of our mother, is itself a beloved wise womb; a womb so wise it embraces and holds our wounds and losses and even our body's death; a womb so absolute that nothing escapes its reality. This womb of Holy Wisdom draws our soul forth to live and work in trust, regardless of what befalls us. We don't plan life, we participate in life, realizing that whatever path we are on this moment is the only path that matters as it is the only path that exists.

> Beloved,
> You are the deep and the shallow.
> You are the fertile as well as the fallow.
> You are the honey and the bitter.
> You are the fire as well as the winter.
> You are the center without any edge.
> You are I am, and I am, too.
> I am your being.
> My soul lives as you.

EXPLORATIONS

1. What are some of your earliest feelings and/or bodily sensations about your life? Take some time to be with them. If they are uncomfortable, stay with them as long as you can, being kind to yourself as you explore.

2. How did you not feel held or seen or cared for—or safe? What feelings arise as you explore these earliest experiences?

3. Identify some of the ways your mind tends to take charge. Explore the role fear plays in your heart as you experience the unpredictability of life. How does your heart feel as you explore? How does your belly feel? What about your head and around your eyes? Listen to your body, simply receiving its wisdom as you explore.

4. Oftentimes spirituality is presented as having to find your correct path. What if the path is attending well to the present moment and trusting the next moment to arise without planning or control? What feelings arise for you?

5. Identify some of the ways in which you do not experience the present moment as a womb of life. Now, identify how you experience the present moment as a womb of life.

Reflection 10

Fishing to Friending

> May you be blessed with good friends,
> And learn to be a good friend to yourself,
> Journeying to that place in your soul where
> There is love, warmth, and feeling.
> May this change you.
>
> O'Donohue, "For Friendship," in *To Bless the Space Between Us*

FISHING

As a young boy growing up in southeastern Michigan, several strong stone throws from the banks of the River Raisin, my dad taught me to fish.

Dad was a teacher, not of fishing, but of high school kids. But he knew the basics of backyard angling—bamboo rod, red bobber, sinker and hook, and the coup de grâce—a nice, juicy worm.

Fishing—setting the bait, lowering the line, and unswervingly (well, sort of) staring at the bobber for the slightest slip beneath the lip of flowing water. We were lying in wait to catch the fish unawares. Our hope was to have set a bait so alluring that the passing trout or sunny would be turned from its fishy business and magnetically drawn to the enticing, wriggling night crawler.

Fishing was about luring and catching the fish before its finely tuned nervous system had become alerted to the con. Seduced, it would disrupt the line in its surrounding of the creepy crawler with its mouth, signified by the slight sink of bobber. Ever alert, we would attempt to deftly jerk back the rod and set the hook in the completely unsuspecting mouth.

Startled by the pain, and driven by millions of years of evolution, the fish would pull back, seeking survival through swimming away as hard and fast as possible. The tug-of-war was on. Our task was to land the fish against its primordial drive for survival. Pull it in against the life force animating its soul. Haul it from the water-home that makes its very life possible. Separate its mouth from the hook. And while the fish was bleeding and wriggling in its final futile gasps for survival, kill it. From fish to *it*. The liminal moment for all animals when "breath becomes air."[1]

Although our angling gear would progress to rod and reel and artificial luminescent bait, seduction into death was the reality of fishing for fish.

METAPHORS MATTER

I recall this story from childhood to highlight the truth that metaphors do matter. Their compressed images contain and convey little (and not so little) worlds of meaning. Metaphors are powerful, because they describe and prescribe our relationships with one another with so few words. The power lies in their awesome capacity to evoke a world. Metaphors can manifest and deepen our sense of Holy Mystery, or they can mask and distort. Oftentimes it is a mixture. But the difference is real, and it matters.

Some metaphors are so woven into our language and story that they trip off our tongue and evoke emotions without thought, without reflection. They carry the pride and prejudice of untold generations of use. We find reassuring comfort in their evocation. Such is the case with the scriptural metaphor found in Matt 4:19 and employed by teachers and spiritual leaders without a minute's hesitation: "And he said to them, 'Follow me, and I will make you fish for people.'"

But if we do stop, recall, and reflect upon this, the actual experience of fishing for fish, the world carried and conveyed by this common metaphor

---

1. A beautiful and powerful autobiography of this transition is Kalanithi's book, *When Breath Becomes Air*.

is neither benign nor gracious. To fish for people? Metaphors matter. To deploy this metaphor as descriptive and prescriptive of authentic and humane human interaction is to draw upon speech that masks and distorts the true expression of boundless love in our relationships. It is a metaphor that masks the distortion of power, masks the distortion of honesty, masks the distortion of the invitation to trust the sacred nature of reality as it already is.

What we are about as spiritual people is not fishing for people. The metaphor matters and is far from helpful.

We don't stand
on the riverbank, the street corner,
or in the sanctuary, the meditation hall, the pulpit,
or on printed page, radio, internet, television,
lying in wait for the unsuspecting person to be caught unawares as they pass by.

We don't set bait to capture human beings against their will.

We don't try to find a bait so alluring that it entices a person away from their own sacred unfoldment.

We don't reel human beings in against their own heart's desire.

We don't seek ways to unsuspectingly set a hook from which another cannot escape without harm to their being—physical, emotional, soulful.

Matthew's metaphor does not travel well across centuries and cultures (and for many scholars the image does not harken back to Jesus). Some metaphors damage more than deliver, and so it is with *fish for people*. The spiritual journey we travel to awaken as Holy Mystery is challenging enough without being given a metaphor that heightens our anxious scanning for dangers, deepens our defensiveness, and reinforces our mistrust.

Authentic spiritual leadership is not about landing human beings bleeding and gasping on the shores of a hungry community—no matter how well intentioned.

Throughout these reflections we have been exploring a very different spiritual perspective than that expressed in this fishing metaphor, which misses and distorts the vital truth that all of us are always already sacred. Each person is already on a journey. It is their own journey. No one, especially a religious leader, should abrogate another's sacred right to discover their own path; authentic leaders do not lure (which is to deceive) to get someone on the path they think is the right one for them. Authentic spiritual leaders have much greater humility (i.e., respect for sacred reality) than that.

Part Two: Unfolding

CONVERSATION AND FRIENDSHIP

Beneath and behind and within the metaphor of *fish for people* is the mistaken assumption that we are here primarily to convert rather than converse. Once we recognize the inherent and integral sacredness of every soul, our response can only be one of longing to converse with the mystery before us. This precious pearl of a person is already a gateway of the infinite. As such, they are the divine grace of invitation to engage in conversation and inquiry. Their presence calls our heart into joyous wonderment. Such conversation gracefully transforms all involved.

Conversation calls us into friendship, and Christianity is a spiritual path rooted in the courageous capacity to befriend another. Here is a metaphor that also matters: "I have called you friends" (John 15:15). The spiritual path is about friendship. In awakening as Christ heart, we realize not only that our being is Holy Mystery manifesting, but this is true of each person we meet. There is both a vertical and a horizontal dimension to human awakening: this is the symbolic power of the cross. At the heart of what John's community discovered in Jesus was Christ's invitation to us to befriend one another (the horizontal). Within friendship is a world where relationships mature through mutual regard, mutual affirmation, mutual compassion, mutual tenderness, and mutual maturation. As we awaken as Holy Mystery (the vertical), we befriend those about us (the horizontal) with curiosity and compassion and joy. Intimacy is infinite in both directions.

Friendship is a metaphor for the spiritual life that manifests the truth of the inherent dignity of every being. Such is the way of Holy Mystery. Friendship is a metaphor that deepens our trust in the experience of the inherent beauty and question that *is* another. Who is this amazing, mysterious gift before me? In friendship, one is not baited; one is not lured; one is not hooked; one is not reeled in against one's will; one does not die as an *it*. In friendship, we meet eye to eye, heart to heart, body to body, soul to soul—deep to deep. We walk toward one another out of mutual trust and affection. Their beauty touches our heart and wonder arises. Through conversation trust is born and matures. We risk, we initiate, we explore, we fail and fall, we rise, we forgive, we love. Through friendship we are transformed in unimaginable ways. Such is the cruciform way of Holy Mystery. In friendship a new kind of world unfolds in which we hold in trust the questioning mind, the searching heart, and the thirsting soul. In friendship no one is killed, but there is dying to smallness and stinginess. Friendship is fruitful and delicious and satisfying, flowing from Christ heart. And friendship matters.

EXPLORATIONS

1. What have been your experiences with being baited, or hooked, or lured, or deceived, by persons in authority? How do you feel as you explore these experiences? (If you have a sense of trauma around any of these experiences, you might wish to find a trauma therapist to help you with your pain.)

2. When the metaphor for spiritual life is that of friendship, how does that resonate with your heart and your body? What have been your experiences with friendship and your spiritual journey?

3. In what ways do you find it helpful, or not, to envision the cross as symbolizing awakening to ourself as Holy Mystery (vertical) and as one who befriends others (horizontal)? Perhaps you have another image that embodies this union of personal awakening and personal befriending? Feel free to explore.

Reflection 11

Holy Mystery's Presence

Ripening arrives to those who consciously breathe
into the well of their confusion and grief,
they shall feel themselves surfacing again with clarity and joy.

Douglas-Klotz, *Revelations of the Aramaic Jesus*

Jesus was a rabbi whose teaching was very much shaped by his experience of what was called the reign of God. For Jesus, this reign, oftentimes called the kingdom, was not a future event, but a reality unfolding here and now. In the Gospels of Matthew, Mark, and Luke, the reign of God is central to Jesus's teaching. But what might it mean for us, living in the twenty-first century, to speak of God's reign? Very few countries are kingdoms with sovereigns; monarchies are a vanishing system of governance. For many of us, kingdoms and monarchs reign mostly in far-off history or fairy tales. Quite often, monarchs resonate within our imagination and lives as antiquated and oppressive, as in the American Revolution's war of freedom against King George III of England.

Biblical scholars Marcus Borg and John Dominic Crossan have demonstrated quite clearly that the reign of God central to Jesus's teaching in the Synoptic Gospels (Matthew, Mark, and Luke) was presented as a liberating contrast to the oppressive reign of Caesar Augustus.[1] I would like to explore another dimension of this teaching and image: the reign of God as a manner of poetic speech Jesus utilized to communicate with others about his very personal and intimate experience of the presence of the Beloved, not only in his heart but as his heart. (Once again, we are encountering the intimate, integral relationship of common good, represented in the scholarship of Borg and Crossan, and the common ground, which we will explore here.)

I'm inviting us to recognize and receive the reign of God as a biblical way of describing Jesus's own awakening as Holy Mystery. His realization that his Beloved reigns in his heart and *as* his heart. Holy Mystery is not a foreign power but the very reality of Jesus's sense of self. Love rules not by fiat, but by being the very spiritual fabric of existence. Love is how Jesus experiences Reality itself and transforms his perspective of God from a tribal deity demanding separation to a more inclusive Spirit capable of converting primal fear into basic trust. There are no limits or boundaries that hem love in. Love reigns in his life, and all life, because love is the spiritual potential of the pearly pearl actualized in history.

We don't have any historical record of those early life experiences that would have nurtured Jesus's awakening process. But they surely did happen, in one form another, most likely from his interactions with his mother and perhaps village elders. What we do have is the story of the maturing Jesus asking his friends to forgive seventy times seven, or without limit (Matt 18:21–22). Or the parable of the prodigal son, where the father's compassion is without condition (Luke 15:11–32). Or the story when Jesus, without qualm or question, receives the tears of a woman that bathe his feet (Luke 7:37–38). Over and again, Jesus embodies loving kindness in situations where others might be triggered by fear to withdraw or judge. As Jesus realizes his own Christ heart, he is discovering God as Holy Mystery who is his Beloved—a holy presence, or Spirit, in which there is no remnant of a judgmental monarch or parental figure sitting on a distant throne ready to condemn. No, Christ heart that has become the center of Jesus's being is the Beloved or Love itself. In Jesus's transformation is revealed what is true for all creatures: each is a beautiful and good portal of the holy presence of boundless love.

What, then, for us, are early childhood experiences opening the heart to the presence of Holy Mystery? What are the qualities of love—of Holy Mystery—as it reigns in the heart? I offer a couple of early childhood

---

1. Borg and Crossan, *First Christmas*.

experiences with my own father, because they introduced me to qualities of Holy Mystery. Perhaps my story will evoke sacred memories of your own.

EARLY CHILDHOOD

When I was about four years old, I awoke early one summer weekend morning and strolled quietly to my parents' bedroom. My mother was already downstairs with her coffee, but with the door slightly ajar, I could see my dad lying peacefully upon the bed, the covers pulled down to his waist to receive the cooling morning breeze through the open window. I tiptoed in, climbed up beside him—not knowing if he were sleeping—and laid my wondering boy head upon the nest of curly hair on his belly. As I ran my little hands through his hair my head floated upon the undulating movement of his stomach, his breath gently coming and going. The sun ever so slowly continued its morning climb, its warmth, like that of my dad's body, melted any distance there may have been between his heart and mine. A golden sense of being one arose, lying pleasurably upon the bed, our single being unencumbered by any edges, expanding endlessly like the soft summer sky of dawn.

This is one of my earliest experiences of realizing union of heart and soul in all its golden wonder. My father was this tender, strong, inviting gate into the endless expanse of the mysterious, vibrant, beauty of creation. I was tasting the gift of being one with the ground of Being in and through the specific being of this young man, my dad. I realized a basic and undeniable goodness in the melting of hearts; a melting that invites us on the lifelong path of letting go and experiencing the golden quality of merging with the Beloved at the center of our own being. I believe that here, in such an ordinary human encounter, is likely the taproot of Jesus's own adult realization that he and his Beloved were one. Most likely, Jesus's own heart melted with his mother's. What matters is that the melting, which flows naturally into the beauty of tasting sweet Holiness, has its source in the extraordinary quality of ordinary hearts that open, meet, and merge.

About a year later, I was with my dad at a football game on a Friday evening in southeastern Michigan. Standing beside him, we were engulfed in an arboreal sea of humanity. As I looked around, I felt as if I were deep inside a forest of giant trees swaying vigorously from a strong current. I sensed myself as tiny, weak, disoriented, and vulnerable. I had no idea where to turn. The next moment I was being scooped up and planted firmly upon my dad's broad shoulders, like a small chickadee suddenly finding a secure perch on a steady oak in a storm. Now, with my skinny little legs within the firm grasp of my dad's hands, I surveyed the scene with wonder. My heart relaxed and my eyes excitedly widened; I had embarked on an adventure. I wasn't simply tolerating the crowd, I was enjoying, even relishing, the excitement. The vital strength of my father's heart was coursing through my body. The strength of his soul was now mine. I knew that *I can do this*. We strode together, as if he were one of Tolkien's Ents bearing a hobbit, with the swaying trees of humanity seeming to part as needed as we wandered about.

Strength—knowing that we can do what needs to be done—is a core quality for developing healthily as a human being. Without it we withdraw and cower and feel we are without capacity to engage whatever is before or within us. Strength is also a quality of Holy Mystery, and it is critical that we have caregivers in our life who introduce us to our capacity to do what needs to be done. Over and again, Rabbi Jesus's encounters with people result in the astonishing realization of a personal strength. Jesus mixes spittle and mud, applies it to a man's blind eyes, and he discovers the strength to see clearly (John 9:6–7). Strength arising from love is solid without being defensively hard. This strength can sway with the wind, flexible in its vibrant sinews. There is a natural give in true spiritual strength. Strong without being steely. Strength with inherent elasticity.

One final vignette. The summer after I turned seven, my parents gifted my older sister, brother, and I with an unescorted train trip from Michigan to Illinois. Illinois may well have been China for me; it was a faraway land that we would reach by rail after many hours. I felt such pride: we had been deemed capable of making an exotic trip without our parents aboard.

The evening before our departure, neighbors joined us for a celebratory spaghetti dinner. As the eating and partying progressed, I found myself feeling worse and worse. I quietly stole away into a corner alone in what quiet could be found. It didn't take long before my mother discovered me curled up. My temperature had soared and my tummy had become exquisitely tender to the touch. Dad gathered me up and drove me to the emergency room. There I sat upon the vinyl-clad examination table, covered by that crunchy white paper in place to ward off germs. The room was cold and sterile.

The doctor probed and prodded and muttered to himself until finally he said to me, "Son, you aren't going anywhere. Your appendix is infected and about to burst. You need to have surgery right away." I sat stunned and crushed, with tears rolling down my ashen cheeks. The adventure had vanished as if it had been a midnight dream. My dad came and stood in front of me as I sat on the table. He held the gaze of my eyes gently but firmly and said, "I think you should be the one to call and tell your mom." Somehow my heart knew that he was right. But even more, I knew, even though I was in tears and heartbroken, that I could do it. There was a powerful peace in my dad's gaze, and it held me and touched me and assured me of my own power to be with what was happening. Nothing was being denied—not the pain, not the sorrow, not the lost dream. It was all there, and I hated much of it; but it was there, held within the power of my little being to endure.

HOLY MYSTERY

Central to our maturing experience of Holy Mystery is the realization of the power to be the truth of what we are within the circumstances of where we are. We are neither dreaming nor fantasizing. We are not idealizing. In this most simple and intimate exchange between my dad and I, he was inviting me to realize and express a power that had been woven into the very Reality of my soul. This power was not reactive. This power was the response of Holy Mystery as me. It was the same power, though in smaller measure, that enabled Rabbi Jesus to accept the cup before him in the garden of Gethsemane. This was an early experience being the *I Am* of Holy Mystery. A taste of Reality. I was realizing through acting in a new way a capacity of strength I had never known before.

Union. Strength. Power. These are some of the qualities of boundless love, of Spirit, present as we awaken as Holy Mystery. They do not come to us magically out of the blue but are introduced to us through the significant experiences and relationships in our life. Our maturation lies in being consciously present to our experience in the moment so that we don't miss the chance when the chance arises. Nature is grace, but we often fail—with no one to blame—to perceive and respond to the invitations that arise in daily life. History is Holy Mystery manifest, but often unrecognized. Our mind, our heart, our body are often elsewhere than where we are. On these three occasions, my dad was graciously attuned to the present moment. I don't believe he himself was conscious of Holy Mystery. But, because his own heart was soft and open, and sincere, love drew his heart and soul to mine in an act of trust in Wisdom to guide us both.

HOLY MYSTERY AND ASHES

What happens when we don't have someone to introduce us to these qualities, or possibilities, of Holy Mystery in our life? We can become hardened, or like ashes, without substance and a victim to the forces that blow us about. Without a sense of union, strength, and power, we can feel unbearably thin and without the capacity to engage life. Like Peter in the Gospels, when confronted with the unknown we can seek the shadows or find ourselves sinking below the turbulent waves of life. We are afraid.

In their book *Proverbs of Ashes*, Rita Brock and Rebecca Parker describe such ashes in the lives of women who experience themselves with no strength or power to act in order to relieve themselves from violently oppressive relationships. To add insult to injury, they find in such language as *the reign of God* religious justification to remain powerless and seemingly disunited from Holy Mystery. They believe they need to suffer the blows and indignities of abuse because that is what they think Jesus did—they have internalized a teaching that the reign of God demands acquiescence. If we suffer like Jesus, perhaps we will then be graced with the chance to rest our heads in peace and know the union we long for.[2] This is a destructive teaching that robs us of our strength, power, joy, and union. All too often this teaching has touched too many of us.

Here is where we need to return to the matter of what we mean by the reign of God, which is a powerfully poetic way of speaking about the boundless, loving presence of Holy Mystery. Rabbi Jesus is a wisdom teacher who invites us to realize a new spiritual perspective, that within our daily interactions we can experience and know directly the living and abiding Spirit that is boundless love—not apart from nature and history, not above nature and history, but as nature and history. There is a depth to Reality we tend to overlook in our habitual ways of skating along on the surface. This depth is the Christ heart of *this* life. This presence, this Spirit, Jesus teaches, can come to reign in our life as our way of living, which means we can come to know Holy Mystery as our very sense of self; as the sure and strong beat of our own powerful heart.

We each need living, breathing, human beings to introduce us to the goodness of life and to the innate goodness of our own being. Jesus is such a human being. There is nothing magical about his interactions, nor those of my father, for that matter. But when those relationships don't exist, tragedy and trauma arise in history as human ashes. Our ashes.

2. See Brock and Parker, *Proverbs of Ashes*, 16–29.

EXPLORATIONS

1. What early childhood experiences can you recall wherein you sensed your true or essential strength, or goodness, or union? Allow yourself time to feel these experiences in this moment in your body. What are the qualities you associate with essential strength, or goodness, or union? If no experiences arise in your awareness that is fine. How do you feel? Sad? Hurt? Angry? Afraid? Confused? Numb? Curious? Listen to your body with gentle curiosity. There is no right or wrong here, only whatever it is that you sense and feel.

2. Were you taught to accept pain and suffering in imitation of Jesus, even if that meant being the victim of abuse? Identify the ways you are a precious pearl, innately good and inherently beautiful as you are. (If you have suffered abuse, which is trauma, you might wish to work with a trauma therapist.)

PART THREE

Worship as Support

Reflection 12

Liturgy
Support for Awakening

Said a disciple to a newcomer at the monastery: "I must warn you that you will not understand a word of what the Master says if you do not have the proper disposition." "What is the proper disposition?" "Be like a student eager to learn a foreign language. The words he speaks sound familiar, but don't be taken in; they have an altogether foreign meaning."

DE MELLO, *AWAKENING: CONVERSATIONS WITH THE MASTER*

RITUAL AND LITURGY AND TEXTS

MOST MORNINGS I GET up rather early, make a cup of coffee or tea, and sit before our windows that frame the trees leading up to the rolling hills of northwestern Oregon. Slowly I awaken, receiving the morning sun, read a little, and then make my way to sit in our meditation room. This ritual is the simple liturgy through which I greet the new day and surrender to my Beloved.

We can appreciate liturgy as ritual done with the intention to hold and support spiritual practice. The liturgy—individual or communal—may be quite simple or complex. We may be brewing a personal cup of matcha or gathering with friends on a weeklong retreat or participating in a formal

Sunday service. The rituals we engage in—from lighting a candle to greeting a friend to sitting in meditation to dancing or body movement—are expressions of our conscious intent to awaken here and now in this moment and devote ourself to Holy Mystery. Such devotion is the heart of true worship. This transforms the ritual into a liturgy of spiritual practice. We are not unaware and moving mechanically through our actions. We are awake. Liturgy is a vessel that holds our practice of worship.

Liturgy not only involves actions—such as lighting a candle, dancing, placing flowers on an altar, conscious breathing, bowing in respect—but also the reading of or listening to stories that frame our actions, teach, and guide us in our practice. Every tradition draws upon sacred stories that are often held as canonical, or authoritative, texts because of the wisdom they convey to generation after generation.

When we are alone or with a few friends it is rather simple and straightforward to choose the texts and the stories we will read for guidance and nourishment. But what happens when we are confronted in a more formal communal worship with a publicly proclaimed canonical text that is homophobic, misogynistic, or simply inherently violent and perhaps terrifying? Most canonical texts of the world's religions are products of a period in evolution when human beings were predominately of tribal cultures with warrior societies. These were overwhelmingly patriarchal cultures that subordinated women and practiced slavery or some form of servitude. The divine was routinely invoked to support the desires of the warrior class and was itself imagined to be and portrayed as a warrior deity, such as YHWH. The divine was a magical or mythical entity existing as a separate being over and above and apart from creation, except for miraculous interventions.

Within Christian communal worship, it is not uncommon to attend a Sunday gathering in which the biblical stories read can land upon us as unacceptably violent. It is vitally important to our awakening that as we engage in our spiritual practice and consider participating in formal communal liturgy, such as on Sunday morning, that the stories we hear be supportive. The process of awakening and surrendering our life is challenging enough without our spiritual communities perpetuating unnecessary barriers.

A basic truth about our soul is that we will only relax and open and receive to the degree we feel safe. If we do not trust the environment we are in to hold us as we are, without judgment and without shame, we will withdraw, close down, and defend our heart. If the worship of communal liturgy is to nurture our heart in devotion to our Beloved then it needs to wisely discern between those stories within its sacred canon that are supportive of the soul's unfolding and awakening as Holy Mystery, and those which are much better removed for academic study, not the least of which is because many attack, judge, demean, and shame.

The standard Sunday Christian worship is particularly challenging for the awakening soul. For instance, although there is much to commend the new Revised Common Lectionary[1] utilized by mainstream Christian denominations, this guide for the use of texts in liturgy does not fully appreciate the important distinction between texts suitable for academic study and those acceptable for worship. As a result, too often a Sunday worship—in a cultural context where organized religion has abused so many innocents—continues to assault the heart, mind, and body of those who have gathered to be guided and soulfully nurtured.

I have lost count of the times members of my communities and spiritual seekers with whom I work have implored why they must continue to be subjected to inappropriate passages and stories. Although such homophobic and misogynistic verses as Rom 1:26–27 and 1 Tim 2:11–14, respectively, are now omitted, they continue to hear passages, which to their ears disturbingly proclaim tribal slaughter (Zeph 1:17–18) and violence (Jer 20:7–13), all in the supposed name of Holy Mystery. These are oppressive texts (and there are more)—painful to read and wounding to hear—and all, as a matter of course, are read as declarations of the word of God, for which listeners are expected to offer verbal thanksgiving.

These are inappropriate texts for worship because they continue to compromise the capacity to nurture the spiritual journey of awakening. They cause the heart to become anxious, defensive, and so retract. As we awaken to Holy Mystery, we need to honor our soul and not allow it to be verbally accosted. The dominant tradition is beholden to liturgical custom that cultishly enshrines a tribal deity whose prejudices, penchants for reactive retaliation, and wholehearted embrace of violence are celebrated in the many pages of the stories regularly proclaimed as purportedly revealing the true nature of Reality. If worship is to provide a holding environment where we feel safe to relax, let down our guard, open our heart, and receive supportive teaching as we awaken, then we must wisely draw upon those texts that support the spiritual journey. There are too many texts which harm the heart, and we are wise to avoid them in our spiritual practice.

---

1. https://lectionary.library.vanderbilt.edu/.

Evolutionary Context

As I mentioned earlier, we have yet to fully appreciate the evolutionary historical context of the cultures that produced the biblical texts we read. We can forget—or have never given it much thought—that texts are products of human beings within specific cultural periods. Sacred texts are those for which the authors and communities make the claim that they reveal qualities of Holy Mystery. Some do not. And some were meaningful for people living in a different age and culture, but not today.

The question we need to ask ourself is whether any particular text is a *wisdom* text: Does a passage have the capacity to foster our soul's growth, helping her to awaken as Holy Mystery, realizing that she is an utterly unique expression of Being that is boundless love? If not, the text isn't suitable liturgical material. This is because worship is essentially itself a spiritual practice, where we gather to experience becoming embodiments of Being in the present moment. We gather for the communal spiritual practice of awakening as Holy Mystery and deepening our devotion to the Source of our soul.

Something we often do not fully appreciate is that part of our soul's maturation includes responsibility for communal, as well as individual, worship. Although institutional authorities believe it is their prerogative to decide on the appropriate liturgical texts, we, as students engaged in spiritual practice, must also decide for ourselves what is suitable. This is a decision we reach as we listen to our heart, mind, and body, and as we engage with others we respect. We draw from the best psychological, sociological, philosophical, theological, and spiritual wisdom we have. We acknowledge the clear truth that not all biblical texts, not all scriptural stories, embody and speak to the boundless love, boundless freedom, boundless wisdom, that is Holy Mystery. We acknowledge that as a species we are evolving and maturing. We realize that our ancestral tribal peoples produced these overwhelmingly tribal texts with their tribal deity. But simply the fact that they have been the community's canonical texts in the past does not warrant their use as liturgical texts for nurturing spiritual seekers today.

Humans of Being

Another way to say this is that there is nothing sacrosanct about the canon from which Sunday liturgical texts are drawn. *Canon* simply means past authorities have given their imprimatur, or approval, to texts. Times change. Contexts evolve. We need to remember that as we awaken we are gradually perceiving ourself and Reality more clearly. Who are we? We are not aspiring to be tribal people guided by a vengeful tribal deity. We are not aspiring to be a homophobic people. We are not aspiring to be a misogynistic people. We are not aspiring to be a racist people. We are not aspiring to be a vengeful people. We heartfully long to awaken as Holy Mystery, being simply and fully humans of Being. We long to be love, through and through, in each and every moment.

Some scriptural passages violate our soul and can be traumatizing. This is not true of the same text for every person. Wise judgment is always in play. This is why the community is always in conversation and why we, as persons committed to awakening, do our best to distinguish between texts for study and texts for liturgy; between stories that sustain the soul, and stories (and prayers and hymns) that sunder the heart. Each of us needs to take responsibility for our soul's unfolding and awakening. Simply because an institution has authorized a text does not render it suitable for liturgy. We need to listen to our soul.

In worship we gather to receive stories that are wisdom for the soul's challenging journey. We need to hear teachings that wisely guide our awakening. We need stories that land upon our soul as nourishment for transformation, such that fear becomes courage, anger becomes peace, apathy becomes engagement, and captivity to survival instinct relaxes into trust of Holy Mystery. There are times when authentic nourishment can be hard to swallow. Our defenses strongly resist change protecting against the loss of our existing sense of self. There is a substantive difference, however, between a challenging text with which our souls must inevitably wrestle (like that of Jacob's heart grappling with itself to know the truth of who he is, or Jesus weeping in Gethsemane as he struggles to abide as his heart) and a text that assaults us in some way. There is a proper season, a suitable place, for the study of difficult and violent texts. (This is one of the primary gifts of a healthy spiritual community.) But that place is not within worship: individual or communal. We come to worship to receive nourishment and guidance for the already-challenging-enough journey of awakening to the truth of what we are.

PART THREE: WORSHIP AS SUPPORT

WORSHIP: COMMUNAL PRACTICE OF PRESENCE

Let's turn our attention now to formal communal worship, such as on a Sunday. When Christians gather for worship; when we assemble for saying prayers, singing songs, hearing sermons; when we come together for Eucharist,[2] it is simply assumed that we are engaging in worship. The last stanza of "An Affirmation of Faith" in the beautifully written New Zealand Prayer Book, states: "You are our God. We worship you."[3] This mostly unquestioned and dominant vision of liturgy for millennia is that Christians gather to worship a magic and/or mythic God, with kindred expressions in both Judaism and Islam. I would like us to explore a different, nondual perspective of worship, reflective of the human experience of Reality in which every person is a human of Being, invited to awaken as Holy Mystery. And a nondual perspective reflective of the human experience of Reality in which an integral dimension of awakening as Holy Mystery is the falling in love with, and the utter devotion to, Holy Mystery. Within this perspective Holy Mystery is no longer an object, magic or mythic, but the love that vivifies our soul and opens her to love the Beloved. Here, love through and through is Reality. I want to be clear that I am not talking about being right or wrong, but of a different perspective, which is nondual, and which I believe is part of the Christian tradition (although neither widely known nor practiced).

Holy Mystery and Jesus

Holy Mystery, as we have been discovering, is not some thing, but how we speak about Reality itself, whose presence permeates all that is as Spirit. Holy Mystery is the beating heart of existence, the spiritual fabric of all things that do exist, and when we gather as community, the devotion of our heart. Presence can be a very helpful word here. Presence is a way of speaking about how Holy Mystery, boundless love, is the palpable Reality of you, of me, and of every creature. (Presence is not a thing, or an object we discover, but the lived experience of love in the moment.) And this is a presence that over time as our spiritual journey deepens, we can actually

---

2. In the Episcopal Church the primary Sunday communal gathering is called *Eucharist*. In many Protestant traditions the gathering is the *Lord's Supper*, while for Roman Catholics it is the *Mass*. In the Byzantine Rite, which includes the Greek Orthodox Church, the language is of *Divine Liturgy*. Other traditions utilize their own terminology with a rich history.

3 Anglican Church, *New Zealand Prayer Book*, 481.

sense and feel in the present moment. The presence of Holy Mystery is not a thought or passing emotion, although it is in both. Presence is one way of speaking about our actual experience of Holy Mystery in our life as love arising and maturing as boundless. We return to that fundamental realization that all that exists only exists insofar as Holy Mystery is its true nature. As we sense the presence of Being in this moment, we are perceiving Holy Mystery in our life and as our life. We fall on our knees, we bow, we raise our hands, we cry, we sing, we sit in utter silence and awe—we worship because of the grace of Holy Mystery. This is the process that is the discovery of, living with, and awakening as Holy Mystery. We perceive Holy Mystery as what we are and the Source of what we are here and now.

The story of Jesus's baptism embodies this truth, pointing to his emerging realization—in biblical poetry—that his loving Abba is his very heart. As he meditates, shares meals, teaches, dances, converses, grieves, his realization deepens and he is discovering Holy Mystery as all in all. His will is being transformed into *Thy* will, which means the preoccupying wants of his daily life are becoming transfigured into the soul's spontaneous flow of living as Spirit. We witness this transformation when the unknown woman enters unannounced into a male gathering to publicly wash Jesus's feet with her tears (Luke 7:37–38). Jesus neither admonishes nor reactively recoils. His body and heart are soft, his mind relaxed and open, and he receives her courageous intimate touch. Day by day, as his own defensiveness diminishes (what we call *kenosis*), Jesus is realizing his true nature is nothing other than Being. He is living with a palpable sense of love abiding as his own self, which means he is awakening as Holy Mystery—not as an abstract concept, or as theological position, but (in contemporary language) as a palpably direct experience of being an authentic person who is boundless love.

Softness, receptivity, nonjudgment, sweetness, kindness, clarity, authentic strength, wisdom: these are some of the qualities of boundless love, of Holy Mystery, that Jesus discovers and comes to know directly and invites his community to realize as well. Jesus's life, his path—and the liturgy of a gathered community—is about the personal realization of Holy Mystery as our Reality. This is the process of our awakening. We begin the basic healing of our heart and the unfolding of our soul. We begin the move from guarded self to spontaneous soul. We not only fall in love with Holy Mystery, but we also awaken to the truth that our own Reality *is* love. Love—the practice of being with the truth of the given moment—is the marrow of the spiritual path.

PART THREE: WORSHIP AS SUPPORT

A Vision

What might worship be for a Christianity become aware that Holy Mystery is Reality? When God language is no longer about some separate particular entity, but utterances of persons become aware that they are humans of Being, as is all Reality? When anxiety about winning a god's salvific favor has ceased to hold relevance? We discover that what matters to our human heart is the soul's unfolding realization: she is simply Holy Mystery manifesting uniquely here and now in this beautiful fragile form. (This Reality, in its own distinct manner, holds equally true for all creatures great and small, sentient and insentient.) We live to love the Beloved, devoting all we are and all we do to Holy Mystery.

Within this vision, Jesus, like Siddhartha, is a wisdom teacher because he has personally realized this truth as his own true nature and the true nature of Reality itself. He has awakened as Holy Mystery. In biblical language, he discovers his Abba as his heart and his heart is utterly devoted to his Abba. Jesus's response is of one who has fallen in love, like a child with her mother, realizing that love itself is the spiritual fabric of life regardless of circumstance.

Just as the realized Siddhartha takes on a new name—Buddha—so, too, does Jesus acquire a new identity in his personal realization—Christ. Both new identities bespeak human beings become fully aware of their own true nature, fully alive, fully human. With each—Siddhartha the Buddha and Jesus the Christ—there is the awareness that their personal realization requires tending, nurturing, struggle, practice, part of which is individual, part of which is essentially communal.

Human awakening requires the support and presence of others in our life rooted in a similar experience and thus committed to a similar vision. And so, Siddhartha the Buddha calls together and forms his sangha, and Jesus the Christ invites his disciples into a beloved community. The call is an invitation to experience the same awakening as the teacher and a life practice of devotion. Practice—both individual and communal—will be the path and means of awakening.

Practice of Communal Worship

Our work as a people, which is one way to describe liturgy, is the soul's practice of becoming the truth of who and what we truly are. *Soul* is shorthand for describing how each creature is Being expressing in a particular place and time. Ordinarily, our soul is contracted by defenses and desires to secure the love it needs to exist; the spontaneity and freedom that is Being is blocked and mostly unconscious. The awakening of our soul as Holy Mystery is learning to live spontaneously as Spirit, moment to moment.

In communal worship, we gather to discover and deepen our consciousness that there is no gap between us and Holy Mystery. Devotion, unlike the worship of a magical or mythical Deity, involves no gap. Devotion flows from a sense of love that knows gratitude beyond belief for the gift of life. Drawing upon Julian of Norwich we could say that peace and love are always in us[4]—because they *are* us—but we do not always act from that love and peace. We become lost, in our blindness (fear, anger, deceit, envy, etc.), to our own truth. We come to worship, in part, battered and bruised by our own inner critic (self-shaming, self-doubting, self-rejecting), attachments, identities, societal prejudices, fears, hatreds—by the effects of human blindness. Worship is where we practice together and directly experience in our practice that, in truth, we are love incarnate longing to live as such. In and through our practice together we are gradually being born into the freedom that is our true nature. We experience forgiveness and healing as unwavering qualities of the Beloved.

As we gather out of complete devotion to Holy Mystery, we hear stories, sing songs, dance, receive teachings, anoint, and are fed. Each of these is a spiritual practice. And this communal spiritual practice is itself more grounded and enriching when it is a receptive listening flowing from the personal practice of meditation. Too much of formal communal worship is busy *doing* and *speaking* rather than relaxed *receiving*, more reflective of cultural anxiety than spiritual grounding and consciousness. Each authentic and sincere spiritual practice within worship flows from emptiness into embodiment such that it sparks wonderment, reignites the fire of soulful longing, and supports us in the gradual realization of Christ heart. The path of Jesus is the soul's gradual awakening to the truth that she is fully alive and thriving, become a living Christ whose heart is utterly surrendered to the Beloved.

Liturgy is no longer the worship of a distanced deity; it now reflects our communal spiritual practice of realizing, as did Jesus, that to be an authentic human being is to be nothing other than the unique presence of Holy Mystery here and now and embody that realization in a life of service, surrender, and devotion to our Beloved in every aspect of life.

---

4. Julian, *Showings*, 245.

PART THREE: WORSHIP AS SUPPORT

WORSHIP: INDIVIDUAL SPIRITUAL PRACTICE OF EMBODIMENT

I have been intimating all along that worship is not only communal but is also individual—and both are integrally personal. Although we may not think of it in this way, worship occurs at home when we light a candle in quiet, sit in meditation, write in our journal, or walk silently and aware through the neighborhood at dusk. This is worship when we intentionally engage in these simple rituals as practices of awakening as Holy Mystery. These are simple yet profoundly meaningful and necessary liturgies supporting our soul's unfolding.

Deepest Longing of the Soul

Before we continue let's take a step back and gain a larger view. A truth-seeking community is one in which spiritual practice is grounded in the love of truth for its own sake and the truth that love is the spiritual fabric of Reality. I do not use the word *truth* in terms of an abstract or intellectual statement of belief. Rather, truth here is experiential, as in what is the truth of your experience in this moment? What are you truly experiencing? Do you feel afraid or relaxed or a little of both? Where do you feel the fear in your body? Does it feel tight? Hot? What happens when you take a few breaths into these areas? Does a sense of relaxation arise? Where do you feel the relaxation? Does anything change? How? These are simple and direct questions about the phenomena of our experience. They are questions that reflect that we are embodied, incarnate, beings—we are a soulbody. It is experience—not supposition, not nostalgia, not speculation, and not belief—that is the immediate and fertile ground of all spiritual practice transforming consciousness, including that of worship.

What this means is that worship does not need to be distorted by either conventional dogmatic religion or creedal belief. Worship can be a powerful source (drawing on word, music, movement, fragrance, architecture, aesthetics) that nurtures our practice such that we feel free to be expressive of the deepest longing of our soul. In the spirit of John's Gospel, this is the hunger to know that Holy Mystery is our Beloved: no gap, no separation—infinite intimacy.

When we begin with this more basic and inclusive understanding of worship as a spiritual practice of gathering to experience becoming embodiments of Holy Mystery in the present moment, we have a liberating orientation. Our attention turns neither to the past nor the future, but the arising present moment in all its power. Here and now is the only place we experience and love our Beloved. We are re-rooting liturgy in the fertile soil of the boundless love of the present moment.

This is worship that has the capacity for universal meaning precisely because it is *not* dependent upon culture-bound creeds; rather, this worship flows from the universal human aspiration to be simply and fully humans of Being awakening as Holy Mystery. In worship we practice—in so many gloriously distinct ways: longing, loving, serving, tender caring, celebration, and gratefulness—that the nature of Reality is boundless love. Liturgy as a spiritual practice is our devotional response to the utter graciousness of life. We see this manifested in Rabbi Jesus's evolving and deepening trust in the presence of his Abba, in many ways finding its fruition in his embrace of clean and unclean, female and male, righteous and sinner, as his friends gathered about the table. This is worship that helps open the gracious eyes of our heart. We are learning to behold one another as gifts, not threats—as companions, not competitors. All are of the spiritual fabric of love that is life.

Awakening as Christ Heart—Parallels and Distinctions

For millennia, spiritual traditions as diverse as Buddhism and Christianity have recognized in their distinct languages that liturgy is a spiritual practice of awakening (within the mystic tradition of Christianity, this awakening is often understood as realizing our self as an embodiment of Being). Nargarjuna, the third-century Indian Buddhist scholar-saint, reminds Buddhists that they live to realize and actualize Buddhahood. In other words, the fundamental work of human beings is the spiritual practice of awakening as a Buddha. That is why human beings exist. In Christianity we live to realize and actualize Christhood.[5] In other words, the fundamental work of human beings is the personal spiritual practice of awakening as Christ heart.

A distinction between Buddhism and Christianity is that, for Christians, awakening is realization transpiring within a spirituality of devotion to the Beloved. Meditation is an integral thread of this personal spiritual practice that is also an expression or form of prayer. The soul is

---

5. In the Eastern Christian spiritual tradition, the fathers speak of the divinization (theosis) of the human being. I interpret this to mean the realization of our Christhood. See Palmer et al., *Philokalia*, 197–207.

Part Three: Worship as Support

communicating—often as silence itself—with Holy Mystery. Precisely because our meditation is purposeful, regular, and not haphazard; because we attend with care to our environment for sitting, minimizing distractions; because we ritualize the start and end of meditation with perhaps a bow, or a bell; our practice is worship in one of its simplest and most significant forms.

To awaken as a Christ is wisdom language for awakening as Holy Mystery: someone whose life flows spontaneously as an expression of gracious Spirit. We look to Jesus as an example of how wisdom spiritual practice can transform our reality into a living Christ. For their part, Buddhists look to Buddha as the paradigm for how to live each moment and be transformed into a living Buddha.

The wisdom path of spiritual practice, represented in both Buddhist and Christian mystic traditions, focuses consciousness on personal experience and its unfoldment. Our personal spiritual practice, which supports our intentional awareness, can express itself in regular practice of meditation, of yoga, of Tai Chi, of Scripture study and reflection, of journaling, of meditative walking or swimming. Within Christianity, this personal spiritual practice is the individual dimension of worship, but that does not mean private. Individual practice is sustained, guided, and challenged by the wider community and the tradition(s). The individual and community exist in a dialectic, where each dimension penetrates and continually informs and transforms the other. We take our personal experiences and share them with our teacher and friends, receiving guidance and support. The community, in turn, receives the leaven of our maturation and questions and sincerity and shares it as a source of wisdom with the wider community.

In the spiritual language of Benedict of Nursia, we are crafting a rule of life to guide and sustain the soul; the rule is really the deliberate creation of a rhythm of wise guidance, whereby spiritual practice is conscious personal liturgy worship, and not incidental and sporadic acts of romantic spiritual forays. The fruition of our spiritual practice is that life-as-worship becomes an actual free flowing of Holy Mystery in all the nooks and crannies of our daily life.

Our personal liturgical life, as we gradually awaken as Holy Mystery in each present moment, becomes a living foundation for communal worship. Without being rooted in our personal spiritual practice, communal worship is reduced to wishful thinking, magical ritual, and nostalgic hoping. When we, as individuals, are sincerely engaged in our personal spiritual practices of awakening as Holy Mystery in our daily life throughout the week, then it becomes possible for the communal gathering of fellow practitioners to be a communal worship that teems with life, authenticity, wisdom, and love. The Beloved, we realize, dwells as the Christ heart of the community as well as our own heart.

EXPLORATIONS

1. Worship is a spiritual practice of gathering to experience becoming embodiments of Holy Mystery in the present moment. How does this resonate with you? What are ways, individual and communal, that you practice gathering? How do you practice gathering your attention? What simple rituals do you find helpful at home to create a space that holds your practice? What communal rituals in communal worship do you experience as supportive? Which ones are not supportive?

2. Have you experienced in communal worship texts that are painful to read and wounding to hear? Take time to breathe into, sense into, and feel your soulbody. What do you discover? How can you honor your soul as you awaken? What support do you need?

3. Have you experienced in communal worship texts that are nourishing to read and expansive of your soul as you hear? Take time to breathe into, sense into, and feel your soulbody. What do you discover? How can you honor your soul as you awaken? What support do you need?

4. In worship we practice longing, loving, serving, tender caring, celebration, and gratefulness that the nature of Reality is boundless love. What are ways your expression in worship as a spiritual practice might become your personal response to the utter graciousness of life?

5. Explore how your spiritual practice of awakening can become a conscious personal liturgy, where Holy Mystery begins to flow into all the nooks and crannies of your daily life.

Reflection 13

Born and Reborn Again

> Return again, return again
> Return to the land of your soul
> Return to who you are
> Return to what you are
> Return to where you are
> Born and reborn again
>
> COMPOSED BY SHLOMO CARLEBACH

WE HAVE EMERGED AND evolved on a planet whose life, or Gaia, is one of seasons. The nature and rhythm of the seasons depends upon hemisphere, proximity to the equator, and many other climate variations. But we are seasonal creatures. The seasons punctuate and orient our life. The winter and summer solstices have captured the human soul and spiritual orientation from time immemorial. It should not be surprising, therefore, that the liturgical life of humanity follows the course of the seasons.

The seasons can be appreciated at their best, I believe, as the continual cycle of life and death, which is also the cycle of being born and reborn again. This cycle is an unending spiral, not a closed circle, with the seasons framing the central moments of gestation of the maturing soul. Worship (individual and communal) is rooted in and guided by the flow of the seasons. Worship midwifes the spiritual journey by focusing the soul upon the process of awakening as Holy Mystery rather than on an external source of salvation from a fallen creation. When the awakening process becomes the leaven transforming the liturgical year, we can discover new, meaningful dimensions in the unfolding pattern of gathering (individually and communally) for spiritual practice.

The Buddha advised his followers to take refuge in the sangha. As Christians, we wisely take refuge in the beloved community. We are social creatures, you and I, ineluctably drawn to each other and the Beloved. Our heart quickens as we gaze into another's eyes and receive a friend's touch. Community is the graceful grit enabling the pearl of life to emerge. Humanity has evolved communally, relying upon one another not only for survival but for enjoyment, creativity, relaxation, exploration, sex, and much more. Our social drive is very strong. When, where, and how we gather makes a tremendous difference in our soul's maturation. An unhealthy family and/or a doctrinally oriented spiritual community can crush the heart. Yet we need family and community. And we need them to be a healthy and supportive presence for our process of spiritual awakening. We do not awaken on our own.

We rely on our spiritual community for support, for guidance, and for love, but also on the wisdom it has amassed over the centuries. This accumulated wisdom, however, is a mixed bag, as we know all too well. If our spiritual tradition is to be a source of wisdom it will need to continually evolve, allowing itself to be transformed by current experiences, insights, and knowledge. Otherwise, what was once wisdom might well devolve into brittle and stale orthodoxy demanding conformity that stifles and strangles the unfolding soul.

If we are to awaken as Christ heart, we need prayers reflective of ancient wisdom, current science, and contemporary experience, continually grounding us in the gracious generative cycle of maturing rebirth. As persons are drawn to gather with others whose hearts simply want to know the truth of who and what they are, we need prayers for communal liturgy that reflect the process of Jesus's own awakening and surrender to his Beloved. Prayers that nurture soulful consciousness and that guide the soul as her defenses thin and dissolve. Prayers that provide a safe holding environment for the soul to rest, explore, open, and receive. Prayers that encourage the loving heart to flow uninterruptedly into care for all creation. Prayers that sustain and nurture a life of devotion for our Beloved who is our Being.

I suggest we would do well to frame the year of seasons and liturgy as the Generative Cycle of life. Gaia is continually gestating, which means evolution is fecund. From the ashes and dust and mud emerge complex living forms—all expressions of Spirit. From the ashes and dust of our anger, loss, and suffering emerge tender acceptance, hope, love, and understanding. Liturgy, when expressed well, reflects not only the seasons of nature, but also the seasons of relationships. Within the Generative Cycle, a community gathers to be grounded in wisdom and to mature into Christ heart. Prayers are the midwifery hands of Wisdom that encourage and invite, but never demand or judge.

Let's begin with an overview of how the Generative Cycle would unfold to guide the soul's journey of awakening as Christ heart. Then we will look at specific prayers for each season of the year.

THE GENERATIVE CYCLE (FROM A BIRD'S-EYE VIEW)

Birthing of New Life

As the winter solstice draws near (which is what the word *advent* means) and the days shorten, with light ever more faint and the night ever darker and longer, the Generative Cycle begins with the mystery of the emergence of new life. The seasonal darkness is the womb gestating hope; this is a liminal night. The darkness is not a cold and barren end, but a new beginning. Fear can be overpowering in the dark, where our sense of sight upon which we rely for life becomes virtually useless. But the loss in acuity of our external sense invites us to turn within and discover an inner sight that perceives clearly in the dark, discovering within a shimmering luminescence. From the classical works *The Mirror of Simple Souls* (Marguerite Porete), *The Dark Night of the Soul* (John of the Cross), *Showings* (Julian of Norwich), and *The Cloud of Unknowing* (anonymous) to the more contemporary *Gravity and Grace* (Simone Weil), *The Path to No-Self* (Bernadette Roberts), and *Luminous Nights Journey* (A. H. Almaas), the birthing power of the womb of darkness has been experienced and explored as gift. We have arrived at the heart, which is a womb, of the Christian celebrations of Advent/Christmas/Epiphany: the mystery of birthing of new life. We approach through darkness (Advent), we receive light in and through the darkness (Christmas), we learn to live from the light of the darkness (Epiphany).

John's Gospel, as well as that of Thomas, captures exquisitely that the spiritual path of awakening as Holy Mystery is integrally a journey in and through birth and death and birth. The birthing process invites us to discover the value of vulnerability and the centrality of trust. We surrender to the dark, silent, empty womb of Holy Mystery, and then find ourself carried to the glistening shores of sunlight and song, filled with pulsating life and brimming with new questions for the journey. Birthing is the movement from emptiness to form, absence to presence, unmanifest to manifest, silence to word, nonbeing to being. And birthing is also the non-movement of form as emptiness, word as silence, manifest as unmanifest, being as nonbeing. Birthing is an undulating dialectic where the light is also the luminous night and the word a silent song.

Awake, O Sleeper

And yet, after we emerge as new beings, we tend to continually fall back asleep, spending much of our life unaware of our heart's deepest longing. Entropy is a powerful force, and we find it manifesting in our unwillingness to persist with our spiritual practices. We begin to coast and with entropy coasting diminishes to stasis, which is its own kind of darkness. Here the darkness can have the quality not of gestating womb but of dying tomb. The heart of spirituality is gradual awakening: Awake, O Sleeper! The spiritual path requires that we wake up from our mechanical repetitiveness; wake up from our survival-driven panic; wake up from our fear-clutched heart and practice living life with open heart, open mind, and open body. We need help with our awakening. Our heart needs the support of a community that is itself on the spiritual journey, not simply going through the motions of ritual long dead. Ash Wednesday, with a renewed focus on our soul's awakening, is a reminder that our body is from dust and returns to dust. (But even dust is of Spirit!) Time on this earth is exceedingly brief. In Holy Mystery there is never divine curse or dismissive judgment. Rather, within the womb of Reality is the opportunity to acknowledge that embodied life is short beyond belief; time is precious. We need to listen in this moment to the longing and wisdom of our Christ heart, awake, and continue our journey.

Transfiguration/Transformation

To embody Holy Mystery means to become translucent, no longer cut off from our unconscious and no longer dulled to the passion of our deepest longing. Just as the earth longs to awaken from its winter slumber, so does our heart. There is this sense deep in our sinews that whatever is inert within us can be transformed and become alive, what is twisted in knots can be loosened and transfigured into beauty. We are in the season, the soulful time, of Lent. Lent is not about self-mortification or denial; it is a time to enter the desert, which means the willingness to reexplore those attachments that derail our soul's growth, driving us through life without consciousness of our true motivations. Lent reminds us that awakening is also transformation. In Lent, we are invited to feel and explore our soul's hunger, our drivenness, and the personality's fear of being alone. Within our hunger, our drivenness, and our fear we experience our arid desert. This is not punishment but gracious opportunity to listen, feel, and respond with heart. The desert is the soul facing itself without distraction, discovering that her true nature is Being, with the inherent capacity to awaken and be alive, pulsating with authentic joy. Within the desert emptiness the soul discovers the presence of Holy Mystery in all that is, even what was thought disfigured and dead. Within the silence the soul learns to listen. Within the darkness the soul learns to see. This is the process of transformation, known in biblical poetry as transfiguration.

Reign of Wisdom

Spring can feel like a fool's hope as winter lingers and the barrenness shows no quit. There are times, however, when the holy fool is the wise one who buoys the soul and reminds us that dance in the midst of death can be an immeasurable gift. Rabbi Jesus is a holy fool whose profligate love confuses and confounds the neat, worldly boundaries of sinner and righteous, clean and unclean, male and female, Jew and gentile. The feast of Palm Sunday immerses us in a liturgical festival of Christ heart whose wisdom, conveyed in reading and song, is learning how to live fully and freely in the world as Being. Yes, death and suffering are indeed in our midst and at times surround us. But they are never all that we are nor the heart of who we are.

First-century authorities—both Roman and Jewish—experience this rabbi's teaching and followers as a threat to the established détente that keeps the fragile peace in this occupied territory. Jesus is aware that his awakening poses a challenge to the ruling order, but the boundless compassion of his maturing Christ heart flows unabated. In this liturgy we can experience anew the courage of being the holy fool who serves and loves truth without reserve, moved by compassion to hold the world's suffering in our heart and respond as skillfully as possible to relieve what we can. Our awakening Christ heart naturally spills over into care of those about us; this world we live in as both sacred (woven into being in love) and precious. This is a feast of the Reign of Wisdom, as we discover that we do not live isolated within a walled-off heart but flow from the Source of all life that is Holy Mystery. We care for those about us because they are us—we are Being. What reigns is boundless love—that fabric of Spirit revealing all of us to be precious embodiments of Being worthy of love and appreciation and life.

Sent to Serve

The Christ heart is a soul of service which flows naturally from being a soul of compassion. In one of his final acts of love, Jesus gathers with his friends and teaches through his own action that the life of awakening as Beloved is a life that pours forth into tender care of others (John 13:1–17). Commemorated in the liturgical service known as Maundy Thursday, the spiritual practice of a life of service is integral to the awakening Christ heart. We are sent to serve, not because of an imposed command (the customary meaning of the Latin word *mandatum*, from which we derive the English word *mandate*), but because compassionate care *is* our Christ heart. Our body is becoming attuned to the unsurpassed beauty of each person and each creature we meet. Service flows freely as our own lifeblood; the human heart is unfettered from the deadening drivenness of guilt, the weight of shame, or burden of requirement. Instead of washing and anointing feet, which bears little meaning for many in contemporary culture, we engage in the simple twofold ritual of washing and anointing hands for tender and courageous service. We are rolling up our sleeves and getting to work in a suffering world that is coming back to life.

It is important to explore a little further the integral role of service within the awakening process. Whether it be Buddhism or Christianity or other spiritual movements practiced in the twenty-first century, a recurring challenge facing spiritual practitioners is a blindness to engagement in the injustice of the world. Another way to say this is that a not-so-subtle dualism can split off the soul from the world, as if there is a tear in the reality of Being. The world becomes viewed as an obstacle or distraction from what is truly holy. In other words, we fail to fully appreciate that we are interpersonal creatures of this evolving cosmos.

The war in Vietnam awakened Thich Nhat Hanh to this hole in consciousness, leading him to develop what is known as *Engaged Buddhism*. He realized that participation in the alleviation of injustice is an integral[1] dimension of spiritual practice and awakening. Having realized the beautiful and healing black stillness of the unmanifest, the soul can be seduced by a desire to withdraw from the hustle and commotion of the world as if this world were foreign to Holy Mystery. There can be the lure to reduce personal awakening to an exclusively interior individualism, where persons became virtually infantile recipients to Reality rather than mature participants with open and receptive souls. There is a world of difference between passivity that awaits magically for change, and an open and receptive participation in life that trusts in the presence of Spirit and is aware of being the embodiment of that Holy Mystery. Today, a real challenge before us is discovering how to participate well in the alleviation of racial and environmental and economic injustices, because they are integral dimensions of awakening as Holy Mystery. As we mature, we realize that the manifest dimension of Holy Mystery (the nitty-gritty of creation) is of equal value and beauty to the unmanifest.[2]

How we serve and whom we serve will depend on our capacities and context. But the soul whose very fabric is love flows naturally to act compassionately for all creatures. Service is the soul alive as love in *this* world.

---

1. In his book *Integral Spirituality*, Ken Wilber helps us to appreciate that there are four basic dimensions to human existence—Intentional, Cultural, Behavioral, and Social. The process of awakening as Holy Mystery includes all four. Why? Because that is manifest Reality in its magnificent fullness. Because love is boundless, there is no aspect or dimension of Reality that is not an expression of love. We can discover that service—engagement in social, cultural, and political life—is not an inconvenient annoyance to the inner spiritual life, nor is it an extrinsic appendage to awakening. Service to this beautiful creation, the incarnation of Holy Mystery, is constitutive to the process of maturing into an authentic human being of Christ heart. We participate in the alleviation of pain of those suffering injustice because we are of the one fabric of Reality that is love.

2. Because Holy Mystery is the Source of all that is, all that is makes a claim upon our soul. An implication, for instance, is that creation, or the environment, is inherently valuable. It is another voice of the Deep singing to our soul with integral beauty. Philosopher Charles Taylor speaks clearly to this moral dimension of existence often overlooked in modernity. *Sources of the Self*, 513.

Companionship and Cross: Mary Magdalene and Rabbi Jesus

As the depth of darkness is really the womb of birth, so too the depth of darkness known in the loss of a loved one is really the womb of new light and life. No one can companion another as they grieve the loss of their infant, their partner, their friend, their parent, as well as one who themself has had to wrestle with the despair and endless tears of loss and only very gradually discover new light in their life. Such light dawns slowly and at the cost of becoming courageous enough to be at a loss and realize one is not at the helm of life. We participate but we in no way control. We learn to treasure true friendship: those who walk beside us without platitude.

As the holy day of Good Friday is ordinarily celebrated, it centers on the theme of betrayal and abandonment. The men flee out of fear and the stalwart Jesus, with his face set against the winds of cruelty, continues forward alone. While others deny, he affirms. This solitary version of the story misses the obvious but overlooked presence of the steadfast women whose Christ hearts reveal the capacity of human beings to remain faithful companions in face of threat and loss. Fidelity and friendship are discovered and celebrated anew as core dimensions of the story of the cross. The spiritual path is one of poverty. This poverty is not an abandonment of companionship, however, but of the letting go of those attachments that obscure our love of the Beloved. The women, throughout the story, are constant in their compassion. They have come to know the truth of who they are and what matters to them. They are women of substance without striving. Their hearts are empty of everything save the same boundless love their rabbi knew. Mary Magdalene and the other women embody the virtues of companionship and constancy with Jesus up to, into, and through his death, offering us an example of awake souls courageous in the face of oppressive cruelty.

Light Renews Our Life

I marvel and relish when the first crocus pops its head up through the spring snow. I hear with simple pleasure the singing of that little titan—the black-capped chickadee—who braves the freezing winter. I smile as the chorus from the spring peepers wafts its way from the ponds through our bedroom window. Entropy is a cosmic force and yet the newness created through evolution is an undeniable power as well. The ice melts and water will flow to the sea and not be utterly thwarted. Life finds a way. Often not as we thought it would in our mind and often with loss. But life finds a way.

Life finds a way and renews us in a manner we never believed possible. Our heart was dead following the divorce. Our life listless and without purpose after our child died. And yet there is more. There is simply more to who and what we are.

The celebration of Easter often focuses on a miraculous bodily resurrection of Jesus. By contrast, our attention is the Light that renews life. One sense of light regards weight and is the loss, the shedding, of heaviness. Throughout his life, Jesus is learning how to release the weight of wrappings and trappings that tended to define him and his need for approval and assurance. With each step his journey wrappings fall away: the woman bathes his feet with her tears and the wrapping of status among the men drops (Luke 7:37–38). His friend Lazarus dies, and he misses his last moments because of being preoccupied with his own ministry. He finds his way to Bethany, but it is too late. Lazarus's warm touch is no more. Jesus's heart falls open and he weeps (John 11:1–44). He sheds the wrapping of self-preoccupation. In the garden of Gethsemane, with his path seemingly at a dead end of failure, again the cleansing tears that dissolve the heart's bindings flow, and his soul discovers that what matters most is *Thy* will, not his instinctual desires (Matt 26:39, 42; Mark 14:35–36). And on the cross, after experiencing complete abandonment his heart turns, falling deep into the Deep of his Beloved (Matt 27:46, 50; Mark 15:34, 37). The wounding weight of carrying a dominating will dissolves. By the time what is left of his body is laid in the tomb nothing remains but the Cool Wind that is Spirit.[3] All that is is a lightness that is light.

This luminous dark of death's silent tomb is the abiding presence of Holy Mystery. This soft light of stars is also found in the tender touch of the women whose hands and eyes and bodies softly brush together as they accompany Jesus in and through his dying. This light, like a lone firefly tucked in the mountain, is within the tomb in which he is laid, which renders this emptiness a womb. The body dies, inevitably, but the Mystery of boundless love endures—that is the heart of Holiness.

Love Through and Through

As spring gives way to summer, we are in the long season of greening. If the renewal of life begun with rains and lengthening days of April and May is

---

3. This description of the Holy Spirit as the Cool Wind can be found in Riegert and Moore, *Lost Sutras of Jesus*, 125.

to take root and bear fruit, then we, like the trees and flowers and grasses, as well as the myriad fauna, practice a way of life that is actually fruitful for the soul. What comes naturally for the flora of this earth for us requires a conscious commitment to a way, a rhythm, of daily life.

The greening human rhythm is in the cadence of forgiveness between lovers after an exhausting spat. The rhythm is the gaze of recognition between mother and son as they knit on the porch in twilight. The rhythm is in eating, sleeping, scratching, and kissing. In this season, the soft light of Spirit slowly suffuses our entire soulbody. Realization is invited to mature into actualization, which means practicing embodiment becomes our very way of living in this world. We awaken not to flee this world, but to become full participants without being held captive by instinctual desire. This is what it means to be quickened in the Spirit, and to be in and of this beautiful yet broken world, but yet be more. Boundless love is never captive. If it does become temporarily imprisoned by our fear or anger or old habits, the soul graciously acknowledges what has happened, smiles, releases, and then continues on. The wisdom of love slowly schools our soul in the precious gift of this present moment. We cannot help but smile. We cannot help but dance. Joy radiates our life, even in the moments of loss. Authentic human embodiment is characterized by Love Through and Through, which is the name of this season. Love is slowly saturating and enlivening every pore of us.

This, in overview, is the seasonal flow of the Generative Cycle of communal liturgy, in which we can rest and receive nurturance to engage in our personal spiritual practice. This cycle creates a safe and fertile holding environment, nurturing our awakening as Holy Mystery. The gaze of our soul is neither toward the past nor the future, but rests gently as the present moment. Rabbi Jesus is embraced not as an exception to humanity but someone who embodies and reveals the human path of awakening as Christ heart. Jesus is who we are each called to be. To be a Christ is to awaken to our true nature, which is an incarnation of boundless love, a manifestation of the infinite unmanifest. Jesus invites us to experience for ourself that love is indeed the spiritual fabric of Reality.

As with Jesus, our own personal journey has its ups and downs, its twists and turns. Our heart is open and soft and vulnerable, and then something in the environment triggers a fear we thought was long gone. We realize that we have more to discover about our heart, our body, and the mental habits of our mind. The Generative Cycle begins again. The Beloved—the

Part Three: Worship as Support

tender presence of Holy Mystery in and as our life—invites us into further soulful exploration. The liturgical community can be a tremendous source of wisdom, strength, and compassion, as the spiraling cycle of birth and re-birth continues. However, the words that the community speaks and sings when gathered greatly determine the degree to which it holds as sacred and nurtures our unfolding journey.

We have a liturgical framework that is generative, what we need also are prayers that are equally so. We turn now to them.

GATHERING PRAYERS OF THE GENERATIVE CYCLE

If the liturgical year is to nurture the spiraling process of awakening as Christ heart, we will need new communal prayers: prayers for gathering our awareness, prayers for gathering around the table, prayers that gather our voice in song. These prayers will be wisdom texts, not petitioning a distant god for some thing, but prayers with the capacity to foster our soul's trust, awakening, and devotion. These are prayers that guide the soul in her realization that she is an utterly unique, lovely, expression of Being that is boundless love. These are prayers that nurture consciousness that we rest *in* and *as* Holy Mystery, accepting whatever our feelings or our soul's state might be. These are prayers that do not try to get us to some place other than where we are, but help us to be with the place in which we find ourself, because it is holy and worthy of exploration and being understood. These are not prayers seeking some thing, but utterances of the heart longing for an intimacy without end with her Beloved.

These poetic prayers gather the community in terms of focused awareness and shared space.[4] We are infusing new meanings into old and sometimes stale words, as well as discovering new language with deep resonance. Let's begin with a melodic, late-nineteenth-century hymn, "Lift High the Cross," and provide new lyrics that support our awakening. The new title: "Robed in Christ's Love."

---

4. More resources may be found on my website, Awakening as Holy Mystery: The Soul's Journey, https://kevingthewforrester.blog/.

Robed in Christ's Love

Refrain:
Robed in Christ's Love,
God's body may we be.
The soul reborn anew,
eternally.

Verses:
Rise from your sleep,
let sloth slip to the grave,
stand tall clothed in Love,
renewed in dignity.

Rise from your sleep,
deceit's dark veil falls free,
stride forth clothed in Hope,
heart's strength is charity.

Rise from your sleep,
fear flees from Paradise.
God's faithfulness with all.
Be Christ. Become the Way.

Words: Kevin G. Thew Forrester (b. 1957)
Music: CRUCIFER, Sydney H. Nicholson (1875–1947)

    These prayers seek to embody and express with clarity, simplicity, and beauty this fundamental truth: we long to be the Beloved's home. A vibrant Christ heart erotically creative while deeply at peace. A tender Christ heart vulnerable and strong, open, and courageous. A wise Christ heart silent and clear, just, and compassionate. A maturing Christ heart questioning and curious and joyful.

Birthing of New Life (Advent)

Lighting of the Advent Wreath

Presider: Holy One,
from whom all life flows,
each moment is a birth,
 a possibility, a hope, a gift.
Soften our heart
to receive your presence
released from the frozen prison of fear.
May we, like Mary,
the mother of Christ,
be full of grace,
and hail your tender love
to a world on edge.

All: **Amen.**

Gathered Around the Table[5]

Presider: God, the Most Merciful, is with you.
Assembly: **And also with you.**
Presider: Open wide your heart.
Assembly: **We lay open our life to the Beloved.**
Presider: May we be a people of gratefulness.
Assembly: **This moment and always.**

Presider: Gratitude, praise, hearts lifted high, voices full and joyful. When we think ourself worth nothing, in truth we are your beautiful body. When we become lost in the maze of belief, in truth we are your heart. When we lose our way or turn away, in truth your presence is constant. And look, Christ, the Beloved, prepares a table for all, offering not just bread, not just wine, but your very Spirit so that we may be filled, forgiven, healed, blessed, and made new again.

---

5. This and prayer on pages 123–24 were inspired by prayers published by Wild Goose Publications. I have greatly revised the originals, replacing the original atonement theology with a spirituality of Holy Mystery.

Presider: Holy One, as we come to share the richness of your table, we cannot forget the rawness of the earth. We cannot take bread and forget those who are hungry. The world is your body, and we are stewards of its nourishment.

Assembly: **Beloved, put our prosperity at the service of the poor.**

Presider: We cannot take wine and forget those who are thirsty. The earth and its weary people cry out for justice.

Assembly: **Beloved, put our fullness at the service of the empty.**

Presider: We cannot hear words of peace and forget the world at war or, if not at war, then preparing for it.

Assembly: **Show us, Beloved, how to turn weapons into tools for harvest, and the lust for power into lives for peace.**

Presider: We cannot celebrate this feast and ignore our divisions. We are one body yet fractured by fear. History and hurt still dismember us.

Assembly: **Beloved, heal your community, in every brokenness.**

Presider: As love you are born; as love you heal, preach, teach, and show the way of life; as love you remain present, even in the face of death on a cross; and as love, after death, you live!

Beloved, present with us now as our very being, our hands and heart are so often full of everything but love. But you are mercy itself and the eternal advent of life being born anew.

So, as we do in this place what you did in an upstairs room, may we know love in these gifts of bread and wine—healing, forgiving, and renewing us as whole; and may we become your gracious Spirit for all creation—loving and caring in the world as the reign of compassion dawns.

Among friends, gathered round a table, you take bread, break it, and say, this is my body, it is broken for all.

And later you take the cup of wine and say, drink and live for I am love even in death. Receive this—all of you—to remember and live as the Beloved.

PART THREE: WORSHIP AS SUPPORT

Birthing of New Life (Christmas)

Gathering Prayer

Presider: The Beloved is with you.
Assembly: And also with you.
Presider: Let us pray together:
Beloved:
Eternal Evening Star,
Deliverer of life,
Redeemer of hope,
Bearer of kindness and love;
You name us—*Sought After;*
You proclaim us—*A City Not Forsaken.*
Our heart sings and sings and sings your love.
for this night, with all creation,
in your boundless love we are born anew
as Christ,
your eternal Word as flesh. Amen.

Gathered Around the Table

Presider: The Beloved is with you.
Assembly: And also with you.
Presider: Open wide your heart.
Assembly: We lay open our life to the Beloved.
Presider: You are life, sustaining and beckoning us home.
Assembly: We sing your love to the highest heavens.
Presider: Creating Spirit,
in you the universe is born,
and manifests your glory from age to age.
You are life, sustaining and beckoning us home.
Assembly: We sing your love to the highest heavens.

Presider: From you pours forth
the surprising unfolding of life:
from creatures of the sea
to the quasars and black holes
of ever-expanding space.

Born and Reborn Again

                You are life, sustaining and beckoning us home.
Assembly: **We sing your love to the highest heavens.**

Presider: You permeate all creation
and if the rocks could find voice even they would
cry out in endless gratitude;
heart, mind, and body,
all reflect your glory.
Yet, as we grow, your presence,
nearer than our own breath,
fades and fades;
we grow blind and long for your face to press
against ours once more;
the song of our heart searches for the Beloved.
You are life, sustaining and beckoning us home.
Assembly: **We sing your love to the highest heavens.**

Presider: We fall. We rise. We betray. We reconcile.
All we do is done in you.
You are life, sustaining and beckoning us home.
Assembly: **We sing your love to the highest heavens.**

Presider: You teach us
to wait upon you in every present moment
and receive your renewal in our life.
You redeem us,
awakening us to know
that because all things are consonant with you,
our soul finds you in all things.
Beloved,
may our heart reverberate with the truth
that your ground and our ground
are one.

Flowering forth as Spirit,
we bring before you
these sacred gifts of your earth.
Holy creatures are they,

Part Three: Worship as Support

      embodying your Spirit,
      as the body and blood of Jesus the Christ.
      You are life, sustaining and beckoning us home.
Assembly: **We sing your love to the highest heavens.**

Presider: On the night Jesus suffers and dies,
      your Beloved takes bread,
      with a heart of gratefulness, breaks it,
      and gives it to his friends, and says,
      take, eat: this is my body, which is being given for you.
      Do this for the remembrance of me.

      After supper Jesus takes the cup of wine,
      with a heart of gratefulness, gives it to them, and says,
      drink this, all of you: this is my blood of our new way of life,
      which is being shed for you and for many
      for the forgiveness of sin.
      Whenever you drink it, do this for the
      remembrance of me.

      God of our ancestors;
      God of Abraham, Sarah, and Hagar,
      Isaac and Rebecca, Jacob, Leah and Rachel;
      God of Jesus:
      Open our eyes to behold your Spirit unfolding in
      the world
      and may the grace of these sacred earthly fruits,
      bread and wine,
      nourish and enfold us forever into one body
      in Christ.

      Eternal Font of life, love, and hope,
      born of your Spirit and renewed in Christ,
      we sing our gratitude
      this day and always.
      You are life, sustaining and beckoning us home.
Assembly: **We sing your love to the highest heavens.**

The inspiration for this prayer lies in part with the beautiful and poignant mystical writings of Marguerite Porete (d. 1310) and Meister Eckhart (d. 1328). For Marguerite, author of *The Mirror of Simple Souls*, our soul finds you (the Beloved) in all things because all things are consonant with you (the Beloved). Eckhart, who was perhaps an acquaintance of Marguerite and possibly even influenced by her teaching, realized that God and creation share the same holy groundless ground—what we are calling Holy Mystery or Spirit.

Birthing of New Life (Epiphany)

Gathering Prayer

Presider: The Beloved is with you.
Assembly: **And also with you.**
Presider: Let us pray:
**Eternal Day Star,
you are the wisdom
for life's journey.
You strengthen the heart
to remain constantly set on you.
You settle the mind
to know true gold amidst a world
of glittering falsehood.
You assure our soul
that the path of Christ's compassion
is the way, the truth, and the life. Amen.**

Gathered Around the Table

Presider: The Beloved is with you.
Assembly: **And also with you.**
Presider: Open wide your heart.
Assembly: **We lay open our life to the Beloved.**
Presider: May we be a people of gratefulness.
Assembly: **This moment and always.**

Part Three: Worship as Support

Presider: Before the beginning
is emptiness and silence.
The Deep sings and
creation arises awesome in beauty.
Christ is the song and
we are the melody.
All that is spectacular, all that is plain,
all that is lovely, all who are loving,
are sung into life.

Grateful as we are for the world we know
and the universe beyond our ken,
our heart sings for the Beloved, gracefully sung from silence.
The Christ song is born upon the breath of Spirit,
infusing and animating creation.
We are grateful for Jesus,
child of Spirit, Christ for creation.
Jesus's compassion changes our heart.
Jesus's clear speaking calms our mind.
Jesus's gentle touch revives our body.
Jesus's steadfast life informs our living.
Jesus's unwavering presence, courageous suffering, fearless dying,
gives birth in our life to Christ, the Life-giver,
breathing healing forgiveness upon all creation.
Therefore, we gladly join our voice with all creatures
as we sing.

Presider: And now,
we fall silent in the presence of Holy Mystery,
the silence that births wisdom beyond words.
Allowing our will and our word to fall away,
emptying our heart and mind,
and bringing nothing in our hands,
we yearn
for the healing, the holding, the accepting, the forgiving, the loving
which alone rests as the silence of the Deep.

~Let us be silent and attentive to Holy Mystery~

> Merciful One,
> our heart is open in gratitude for your Spirit
> kindly arising as this bread and wine,
> Christ food for all who gather.
> May we know that same Spirit as our soul,
> converting us from the patterns of this passing world,
> until we awaken as Christ heart, food for the world.

Awake, O Sleeper (Ash Wednesday)

An Opening Acclamation

Presider: Awake, O sleeper.
Assembly: **The reign of mercy now dawns.**
Presider: Blessed be the Most Merciful.
Assembly: **Our health, our hope, our life.**

Gathering Prayer

Presider: The Beloved is with you.
Assembly: **And also with you.**
Presider: Let us pray:
> **Beloved,**
> **you are present within us**
> **as a fire burning in our heart:**
> > **burn away the shame that imprisons our soul;**
> > **burn away the rage that drives us to vengeance;**
> > **burn away the fear that despairs of your love.**
>
> **Leave nothing buried in our ashes,**
> **but Christ heart alive as you. Amen.**

An Invitation to the Lenten Journey of Transfiguration

Presider: Dear Friends, so very often our mind is anxious about what might come our way and our heart is troubled with sorrows and losses we have known in days past. Being pulled fore and aft, our soul finds no still place to land, no ground upon which to rest.

We long to learn how to live in this present moment, the only moment in which the Beloved is to be known. All too often we feel trapped by anxious mind and fearful heart as we search for freedom.

Lent invites us to discover that now is the season to realize that we and the Beloved are one. The place of rest we seek is the Spirit of our very soul, and this Spirit calls us to trust and settle into this moment.

To return to Spirit is to discover anew the land of our soul and to live the unfolding life of transfiguration. We are learning neither to cling to nor reject anything—thought, memory, desire, sorrow, longing, frustration, loss. The land of our soul is the silent Spirit from which all life arises and passes as dust upon the wind.

What thoughts stir your mind this day into an anxious whirlwind? What memories hold your heart tightly captive in sorrow? What is capturing your soul, blinding her to the grace arising this moment before you?

Freedom is the fruit of courage. Not the false courage to deny or destroy. Not the false courage to push through or pull away from. But the courage to consider and honor and receive how you are exactly this moment—whatever that might be—and to offer all upon the altar of your heart.

As you renew your Lenten journey this day, become aware of the thought that troubles your mind; remember the loss that weighs upon your heart; attend to the love that moves your soul; and offer all to the holy flame that burns upon this sacred ground.

Silence.

Presider: Silent Spirit of Beloved and soul, eternal flame of all that is and that shall be, all creation arises as beautiful dust of the earth. Grant that these sacred ashes—holy remnants of thought and desires of heart—may be to us a sign of our body's mortality; may they remind us that time is short and passes ever so swiftly. We must not tarry. Resurrection today is the most precious gift. Now is the time to awake and receive from the Spirit the life of Christ.

All: **Amen.**

Presider: Remember that your body is dust, and to dust it shall return.

Gathered Around the Table

Presider: God is love and love is you.
Assembly: **And also you.**
Presider: Love moves our joyous heart
Assembly: **To rest all creation in the Beloved**
Presider: Our soul cries out with thanks.
Assembly: **We live in God alone, for nothing else remains in love's bright burning.**
Presider: As daughters and sons of Zion,
we neither desire
nor despise "poverty nor tribulation,
neither mass nor sermon,
neither fast nor prayer."
Assembly: **We give all that is necessary,
without remorse of conscience.**
Presider: For love transforms our soul
into a "student of divinity,"
where we sit "in the valley of humility
and on the plain of truth,
and rest on the mountain of love."[6]
Assembly: **And because all things are consonant with God,
we find God in all things.
We have become joy itself,**

---

6. Porete, *Mirror of Simple Souls*, 87.

                swimming in the "sea of joy."[7]
Presider: As joyous fire and flame of God,
                our heart sings forth love's praise.
Presider: Every attachment
                deprives us of the freedom
                to wait upon God
                in the surprising moment of now.
Assembly: **Trapped by anxious mind and fearful heart**
                we search for someone to blame.
                We feel as if we have fallen from grace
                and are lost from the holy truth
                of life cradled in love.
Presider: We become convinced
                that we are set apart from love,
                      guilty,
                            judged,
                                  and shamed into suffering souls.
Assembly: **In desperation we condemn others**
                and seek release in the delusion of revenge.
Presider: Yet the sea of joy washes upon us
                with relentless tenderness,
                bearing our lifeless soul
                across the Red Sea.
                With our own wrath
                drowned in Christ,
                our soul lives through the purity
                of the unity
                of the will
                of God
                that encloses all creation.

Presider: With Christ,
                the Beloved,
                our heart now knows:
All: **There is no one except Christ,**
                no one loves except Christ,
                for no one is except Christ,

---

7. Porete, *Mirror of Simple Souls*, 109.

	and thus Christ alone loves completely.[8]
Presider:	Life is a banquet
	flowing from the heart of the triune God:
	"Lover, Loved, Love."[9]
	Jesus is now ash from the lover's fire.
Assembly:	**Christ alone remains,**
	inviting all to the table
	spread upon the sea of life.
Presider:	Mind, heart, body:
	all is an open banquet.
Assembly:	**No walls exist—**
	the shimmering face of the lover
	cradles our countenance and says:
Presider:	Receive, eat.
	This is my body, I am for you.
	Remember, you can be no less for me.
Presider:	Freely, the loved pours forth his life.
	This soul is free,
	"supremely free,
	in the root,
	in the stock,
	in all her branches
	and all the fruits of her branches."[10]
Assembly:	**Nothing but sweet flowing wine remains**
	and the soul says:
Presider:	Drink this, all of you:
	I am life,
	I am mercy,
	I am joyful forgiveness.
	Remember, you can be no less for me.
All:	**Through Love and with Love and in Love,**
	in the unity of Holy Love,
	we live as the Beloved's,
	for ever and ever. AMEN.

---

8. Porete, *Mirror of Simple Souls*, 167.
9. Porete, *Mirror of Simple Souls*, 184.
10. Porete, *Mirror of Simple Souls*, 160.

PART THREE: WORSHIP AS SUPPORT

Transfiguration/Transformation (Lent)

Gathering Prayer

Presider: The Beloved is with you.
Assembly: **And also with you.**
Presider: Let us pray:
**Sovereign of my heart,
Home of my soul—fertile ground of life,
your Spirit cries out to your famished ones:
return to the land of your soul,
for it flows with milk and honey.
When you would hunger for bread,
remember that I alone fill your soul.
When you would be prostrate before power and glory,
remember that I alone satisfy your soul.
When you would reject life's sorrow and seek me only in safety and security,
remember that the land of your soul is the ground Christ treads.
Return to the land of your soul. Amen.**

Gathered Around the Table

Presider: The Spirit is with you.
Assembly: **And also with you.**
Presider: Open wide your heart.
Assembly: **We lay open our life to the Beloved.**
Presider: May we be a people of gratefulness.
Assembly: **This moment and always.**

Presider: Before there is time or place or word,
emptiness is Reality.
The fathomless Silence—
source of word and world,
and all that comes to be—
bursts forth from the womb of the holy Deep,
flowing without shore as the sea of boundless love.
As Silence speaks,

the song of Holy Mystery brings forth all creatures of the earth,
giving breath to humankind.
Wondrous are you, Holy One of Blessing.
All that arises is a sign of hope for our journey.
And so, as the morning star sings your praise,
we join all creation as we
shout with joy.

Presider: Beloved,
you speak even in silence, even as silence;
you call a people home, as a light to the nations,
you deliver them from bondage
and lead them to a land of promise.

Of your gracious Deep, Jesus is born,
sharing the fullness of life,
proclaiming your Spirit as the reign of love,
and giving himself to all, a fragrant offering.
In the path of Jesus,
we realize freedom from the blindness of sin,
we awaken as Christ heart and live as you.

We are grateful that on the night before he dies
Jesus takes bread,
and with a heart of gratefulness, breaks it,
gives it to his friends and says:
Take, eat, this is my body, broken for you.
Live as I have lived.
After supper Jesus takes the cup of wine,
says the blessing, gives it to his friends and says:
Drink this, all of you:
from this cup flows life.
Live as I have lived.

And so, aware of your love in this moment and present
in friendship, tenderness, mercy, death, and life;
knowing Christ as the lifeblood of creation;

> transfigured through your Spirit;
> we lay before your heart these gifts,
> drawn from the sacred earth and worked by human hands.
>
> As creatures of your Spirit,
> may our heart open to receive
> these gifts of bread and wine
> as the Body and Blood of Christ.
> Grant that we, burning with the Spirit's power,
> may be a people of hope, justice, and love.
>
> Source of life, draw us together as the body of Christ,
> and in the fullness of time, which is this gracious moment,
> gather us with blessed Paul of Tarsus and Marguerite Porete,
> and all people into the joy of our true home.
>
> Through Christ and with Christ and in Christ,
> by the inspiration of your Spirit,
> we abide in your boundless love, now and always.

All: **Blessed are you now and for ever. AMEN.**

This prayer speaks of the Reality of Holy Mystery permeating all that is, for all that is exists only insofar as Spirit (Being) is the animating force. Yet it is also true that our sense of our true nature fades in our maturation as individuals. We become identified with our various idealizations, defenses, passions, avoidances, which commence the search as adults for the truth of our soul. Spirit's presence is life never ceasing to sustain and beckon us home here and now. Home is Christ heart. Whatever we do is done in the Spirit and so we are moved to devote our life to the Source of all.

Reign of Wisdom (Palm Sunday)

Gathering Prayers

Presider: Our heart knows only this song of love,
Wondrous One,
for the acts of compassion by which you call us home
through Christ.
On this day Jesus enters the holy city of Jerusalem in triumph,

	and is proclaimed as King of kings
	by all who are utterly foolish of heart.
	These branches hail the power of love.
	May we who bear them
	ever receive the wisdom of Christ,
	and follow the Beloved's way as the path of life.
All:	**Amen.**

Presider: The Spirit is with you.
Assembly: **And also with you.**
Presider: Open wide your heart.
Assembly: **We lay open our life to the Beloved.**
Presider: Let us cry out:
All: **Hosanna in the highest!**
Presider: No longer are we weighed down
by our small notions of right and wrong;
Assembly: **Wisdom has built her home of our heart.**
Presider: No longer are we buffeted about
by passing thoughts and fleeting emotions;
Assembly: **Wisdom stands solid as a mountain, our very soul.**
Presider: No longer are we consumed
by vain pursuit of false gods to confirm self-worth;
Assembly: **Wisdom is the wondrous Guest we have longed for all our life.**
All: **Blessed is the One who reigns.**
Hosanna in the highest! Amen.

Gathered Around the Table

See above, Transfiguration/Transformation (Lent)

Sent to Serve (Maundy Thursday)

Gathering Prayer

Presider: Let us pray together:
Beloved, life is a banquet overflowing
from the heart of your dance of love.

On this night, Jesus is now ash from the lover's fire and Christ alone remains,
who invites all to the table spread upon the sea of generosity.
Freely, love pours forth life.
This Soul is free, supremely free,
   in the stock,
      in all her branches
         and all the fruits of her branches.
Nothing but sweet flowing wine remains
and the Soul says:
Drink this, all of you:
this is my life blood
a joyous covenant
from which flows forgiveness of sin and life renewed.
Remember, you can be no less for me. Amen.

Washing and Anointing of Hands for Service

Presider: Jesus ate with his disciples and washed them.
Afterward, he said:
Do you know what I, your teacher, have done to you?
I have given you an example, that you should do as I have done.

Assembly: **Peace is my last gift to you,**
my own peace I now leave with you;
peace which the world cannot give, I give to you.

Presider: I offer you a new path:
love one another as I have loved you.

Assembly: **Peace is my last gift to you,**
my own peace I now leave with you;
peace which the world cannot give, I give to you.

Presider: By this shall the world know that you are my disciples:
that you have love for one another.

The priest/leader washes participants hands in the font and says:

Presider: You are washed by Christ in the waters of baptism.

Born and Reborn Again

The deacon/leader anoints participants hands with oil and the sign of the cross and says:

Deacon: These are the hands of Christ, anointed for service.

Gathered Around the Table

Presider: The Spirit is with you.
Assembly: And also with you.
Presider: Open wide your heart.
Assembly: We lay open our life to the Beloved.
Presider: May we be a people of gratefulness.
Assembly: This moment and always.
Presider: It is truly good and joyful,
to open our heart in thankfulness
to the graceful source of life and fountain of mercy.
All creation is a blessing
that nourishes with constant love;
in gratitude we lift our voices together in song.

Presider: Blessed are you, gracious One,
source of the universe and font of life.
We are your image
as we embody your boundless love.
You place the world into our care
that we might be your faithful stewards
and show forth your bountiful grace.
Although we try, we do often fail to honor your image
in one another and in ourself;
we often do not see goodness in the world around us;
afraid, we violate creation,
abuse one another and reject your love.

Yet, Beloved, you never cease to care for us
and prepare the way of life.
Through Abraham and Sarah and Hagar,
you call us into covenant.
You are freedom from slavery.

Part Three: Worship as Support

You are the path through the wilderness.
You are the heart of the prophets
whose voice is light in the darkness.

When the moment is ripe and ready,
Jesus is born and dwells among us.
Jesus, the Life-Giver, reveals your Spirit as love.
As the Unified One,[11] Jesus is Christ,
your heart is his, your will his path:
> love without condition and mercy without end,
> even as it costs his life.

On the night before he dies,
the Life-Giver takes bread,
and with a heart of gratefulness
he breaks it, gives it to his friends, and says:
Take, eat: This is my body which is being given for you.
Live as I have lived.
As supper is ending, the Life-Giver takes the cup of wine,
and with a heart of gratefulness gives it to them, and says:
Drink this, all of you: this is my blood of the path of love,
which is being poured out for you and for all.
Live as I have lived.

This bread and wine are holy gifts of a holy creation,
woven into being by the Spirit.
May we receive these gifts as Christ for Christ,
> drawing us forth into lives of compassion and justice in a suffering world.

Beloved, teach us to dwell with N and all your saints
in this moment that is your reign of mercy and love and justice.

Through Christ and with Christ and in Christ,
in the unity of the Holy Spirit,
may the Beloved be our life, this day and always. **AMEN.**

---

11. Life-Giver and Unified One are translations of the Syriac Mahyânâ and Iḥidaya, respectively.

Companionship and Cross: Mary Magdalene and Jesus (Good Friday)

Gathering Prayers

Presider: Blessed be the Beloved,
Assembly: **Forever and ever. Amen.**
Presider: Beloved,
we, your very own,
born of your Spirit
and called to awaken as your heart,
are blinded by ignorance, fear, anger, and greed.
This sinful veil blinds us
to your beauty embodied in neighbor and creation.
We stand before you
with your mercy raining down upon us,
washing over our lives with renewing forgiveness.
Be the grace that strengthens us to serve in newness of life.
All: **Amen.**

Presider: Let us pray together:
Gracious One,
turn the gaze of our soul to the Beloved,
heart of our heart,
whose beauty is broken open upon the cross:
may Christ's arms embrace our broken life;
may Christ's heart heal our tortured world;
and may the sinful veil
of ignorance, fear, anger, and greed
be lifted from our eyes,
so that we might see and fall
into the Beloved's boundless mercy. Amen.

The Passion: Companionship and Cross[12]

Reader: The Passion of Jesus and Mary

---

12. This liturgy was inspired by material in Bourgeault, *Wisdom Jesus*, ch. 9.

Part Three: Worship as Support

Gathered with his friends, "the Blessed One said, Peace be with you! Bear my peace within yourselves! Beware that no one lead you astray saying, 'Look over here!' Or 'Look over there!' For the Child of Humanity is within you! Follow it! Those who seek it will find it."
~Gos. Mary 4:2–7 *NNT*

Jesus also said, "Do not let your hearts be troubled." Later, he was arrested, tortured, and hung on the cross by the Romans. Near the cross of Jesus were standing his mother and his mother's sister, as well as Mary the wife of Clopas and Mary of Magdala.
~John 14:1a; 19:25–26a

Jesus gave a loud cry and breathed his last.... And the women looking on from a distance included Mary Magdalene and Mary, the mother of James the younger and of Joses, and Salome.
~Mark 15:37, 40

Joseph of Arimathea took the body, wrapped it in a clean linen sheet, and laid it in his newly made tomb, which he had cut in the rock; and, before he left, he rolled a great stone against the entrance of the tomb. Mary of Magdala and the other Mary remained behind, sitting in front of the grave.
~Matt 27:59–64

On the first day of the week, when it was still dark, Mary Magdalene and the other Mary brought spices to anoint Jesus. But the stone was gone, and he was not there. An angel of the Lord said, "Do not be afraid. I know you are looking for Jesus who was crucified. He is not here; for he has been raised, as he said. Come, see the place where he lay." Go and tell the others.
~Matt 28:1–9; Luke 24:1–3

Jesus himself appeared first to Mary Magdalene, but she did not recognize him.
　~Woman, why are you weeping?
　~Sir, if you have carried him away, tell me.
　~Mary.
　~Rabbouni!
　~Mary, do not hold on to me. . . . Go and tell the others.
Mary Magdalene went and announced to the disciples, I have seen the Lord!
~John 20:14–18

Born and Reborn Again

Wherever the good news is proclaimed in the whole world, what she has done will be told in remembrance of her.
~Mark 14:9

Meditation—The Wisdom Way of the Cross

Presider: Jesus—
>open arms,
>>open table,
>>>God's love embracing all.

               Jesus—
>love of God,
>>love of neighbor,
>>>no compromise, no condition,
>>>>Rome's cross.

Assembly: **Come. Let us awaken as Christ heart and follow love's wisdom way.**

We may come forward in silence and light a candle beside the cross.

Solemn Prayers

Presider: Dear people:
Jesus of Nazareth and Mary Magdalene,
his beloved companion,
embody the Wisdom way of life.
Their selfless companionship
reveals the path of life
to all who would see and receive.
This path is the light of life
amid isolation, suffering, darkness, and death.
Born of Holy Mystery,
we, too, are companions in Christ.
We, too, are life-givers.
We, too, are heirs of everlasting life.
We pray with gratitude, therefore, for people everywhere.

Part Three: Worship as Support

Presider: Let us pray in thanksgiving for those in communities committed to the path of love and all who seek to restore wholeness amid suffering:

> For unity in witness and service
> For all teachers and leaders
> For all members in this community.

With grateful hearts that each soul is the presence of Holy Mystery and the offer of love and peace.

~Singing bowl or bell sounds

All: **Beloved,**
your Spirit,
source of life and hope,
weaves us together as one body,
dwelling as you.
Our self, our soul, our body,
are your very presence.
We offer all we are to the path of awakening as Holy Mystery.
Be unto us this day the path of life,
so that all that we are
and all that we do,
serves all we meet.
Amen.

Presider: Let us pray in thanksgiving for all nations and peoples of the earth, and for those in authority;

> For N, the President of the United States
> For the Congress and the Supreme Court
> For the Members and Representatives of the United Nations
> For all who serve the common good.

With grateful hearts that as we awaken our life is every more fully committed to justice and truth, peace, and concord.

~Singing bowl or bell sounds

All: **Beloved,**
we are grateful
for the flame of Spirit

**that ignites hearts to awaken as Holy Mystery and
to burn for justice and peace;
for the light of Holy Wisdom
that guides our mind in compassionate counsel
for the nations of the earth;
may the fire of Holy Love so consume the dross of our life
that nothing remains on earth or in heaven
but Christ,
all in all. Amen.**

Presider: Let us pray in thanksgiving for all who suffer in body, heart, or mind;
>> For the asleep and wandering
>> For the hungry, homeless, destitute, and oppressed
>> For the sick, wounded, and impaired
>> For those in loneliness, fear, and anguish
>> For those driven by doubt or despair
>> For the sorrowful and bereaved
>> For prisoners and captives, and those in mortal danger.

With grateful hearts that Mercy is comfort and relief, and that knowledge of love stirs up in us the will and patience to minister to the needs of our sisters and brothers.

~Singing bowl or bell sounds

All: **Beloved,
Source of all creation,
comfort of all who sorrow,
strength of all who suffer:
May those in misery and need
discover mercy present within them
in all their afflictions.
Be unto us the constancy that steadies our soul
to persevere in service to all in need,
for all indeed are Christ. Amen.**

Presider: Let us pray in thanksgiving for all who search for God;
>> For all of us distracted by sloth
>> For all of us consumed by anger

> For all of us swollen by pride
> For all of us misled by deceit
> For all of us obsessed by envy
> For all of us driven by greed
> For all of us trapped by fear
> For all of us deceived by gluttony
> For all of us hounded by revenge.
>
> With grateful hearts that God opens all hearts to unfolding truth.

~Singing bowl or bell sounds

All: **Beloved,**
Let us commit ourself to the wisdom way.
Let us open our heart to receive the grace of a holy life.
Let us come to know the fullness and joy of Christ.
In birth we are born in Christ.
In death we die in Christ.
In resurrection we live as Christ.
All is given by you
as a taste of the Christ.
May we joyously receive. Amen.

~Singing bowl or bell sounds

Presider: Beloved,
"Everything looks to you, without thinking.
Shower us with your Healing Rain!
Help us to overcome, give life to what has withered.
And water the roots of kindness in us."[13]

All: **Amen.**

Light Renews Our Life (Easter)

Gathering Prayer

Presider: We are one body and one Spirit;
Assembly: **transfigured in love;**
Presider: we are one heart and one life;

---

13. Palmer, *Jesus Sutras*, 204.

Assembly: sent forth in love.
Presider: Let us pray together
**In water are we conceived.
In water are we knit together in the Spirit.
Through the breaking of water are we born.
Through the drinking of water are we nourished.
You, O Beloved, are the living water:
wash over us, again and again and again,
that in Christ we might live as your daughters and sons,
and that with Christ as our heart
we might respect the dignity of every human being. Amen.**

Gathered Around the Table

See above, Birthing of New Life (Christmas)

Love Through and Through (Season After Pentecost)

Gathered Around the Table

Presider: The Spirit is your life.
Assembly: **And also yours.**
Presider: Give unto the Beloved your heart, your mind, your body.
Assembly: **With thanks and praise, we lay open our life.**

Presider: How good and joyful it is
always and everywhere to give thanks,
Beloved.
As Christ we live and in the Spirit we love,
united with all peoples in our thirst for what is true.
We are here to serve as we care for creation,
living a gospel of gracious hospitality and healing justice.

And so, with hearts overflowing in gratitude,
our voices join with all creatures as we sing.

Presider: Holy and gracious Mystery,
we are yours, body and soul—

Part Three: Worship as Support

even in our blind complacency with evil and our fear of death.
You are mercy itself,
embodied in the tenacious and tender life of Jesus become Christ—
> sacrament of eternal and undying love.

Jesus is who we are each called to be: love, through and through.

Jesus willingly stretches out his arms upon the cross,
refusing to compromise his compassion,
offering himself
as the way of reconciling love for the whole world.
On the night the Romans arrest, torture, and kill him,
Jesus takes bread;
with a heart of gratefulness,
he breaks it, and gives it to his disciples, and says,
> take, eat: this is my body.
>> Become who you receive.

After supper Jesus takes the cup of wine;
and with a heart of gratefulness,
he gives it to them, and says,
drink this, all of you: this is the blood of the new life:
> a life of hospitality—for none are turned away;
>> a life of forgiveness—for mercy has no end;
>>> a life of friendship—for we love even our enemies.
>>>> Drink this cup, for the blood of new life flows through you.

Becoming love, through and through,
we celebrate the gift of our eternal life as Spirit.
Living as Christ's resurrected body, our hearts ascend,
holding in open arms these precious and sacred gifts,
blessed by Spirit
as the holy food and drink
of new and unending life as Christ for the world.
As the blood of new life

flows through our heart and cleanses our soul,
may our heart overflow in service, this moment, and each moment,
in unity, constancy, and peace;
for now is the reign of mercy—
now you are life, now you are love,
through and through.

All: **AMEN.**

This prayer, for what is usually the season after Pentecost, draws upon the intimate language of marriage: *we are yours, body and soul*, reflecting the truth that awakening is the realization of intimacy as infinite. This abiding truth perdures even when we find ourself complacent and complicit with evil, as well as in our fear of death that so often leads us to seek refuge in defense. Holy Mystery is *mercy itself*. This is no longer mercy experienced as noble deference to a threatening deity. This is the mercy lovers' hearts extend one another embodying the sweetness of loving-kindness amid betrayals small and large. Mercy here is a dimension of our true nature: *Love, through and through*. Just as Jesus awakening to the Reality of being a creature of love, we, too, are invited to awaken to the same truth of who we actually are in this life; indeed, to become Love, through and through is to awaken as Holy Mystery and is why we exist as human beings. This prayer also draws upon that traditional language of *sacrament*, utilizing it as a synonym for embodied Spirit. In this sense, all creation is sacrament, for all that is exists as a manifestation of Holy Mystery.

We are at the dawn of a new age of the continually unfolding Christ movement. We need new prayers reflective of mature personal and communal spiritual practice. We need prayers offered by those whose own being is marinated fully in the Mystery of Spirit; prayers that embody eternal wisdom for today; prayers animated by the existential flame of truth. Prayers that support and nurture awakening as Holy Mystery. These are joyful waters to play in.

EXPLORATIONS

1. Which prayers above resonate most with your heart? Mind? Body? How do they support, or not, your awakening as Holy Mystery?

2. Try writing your own prayer for one or more of the seasons of the year. Keep the words as simple as possible, allowing your soul to speak straight from the heart. Incorporate the prayer into your daily rituals of liturgy or share it with friends to pray together. Try reading aloud your prayer(s) with others as practice of faith explorations, discovering what questions, confusions, wonderings, arise.

3. If you are drawn to communal liturgy and do not find a community that is supportive, explore possible ways of gathering with others who are supportive.

Reflection 14

Grateful and Communal Creatures

Everything is a gift.
The degree to which we are awake to this truth is a measure of our gratefulness,
and gratefulness is a measure of our aliveness.

Gratefulness is the great task,
the how of our spiritual work, because, rightly understood,
it re-roots us.

DAVID STEINDL-RAST

WHEN YOU GAZE UP into the night sky, perhaps from the satin darkness of a remote mountain park, or the cozy vestibule of your backyard, what do you see? Pinwheeling galaxies? Endless expanse of interstellar space? Familiar special neighbors such as Orion or Ursa Major?

Whatever your eyes behold is usually received through story, probably intertwining and commingling narratives. A story of 13.8 billion years of expanding evolution whose ancient light is landing just now upon your retina. A story of cosmos-as-creation, dynamically unfolding, moment to moment, each arising a surprise, and replete with mystery. For some, this is a narrative of the power of pure chance at work on both cosmic and microcosmic scales; for others, a story of the bodying forth of Holy Mystery in which form emerges from the emptiness. Yes, chance is at play but within the wider and deeper Reality of love.

When the beauty of evolution is received and understood within the larger, or metanarrative of manifesting Spirit, what we behold when we truly behold anything is the embodiment of Holy Mystery. Spirituality and science are twin offspring of the same mother—the dynamic Reality of Being—offering complementary understandings and appreciations of Reality. Without spirituality, science can readily devolve into a scientism that flattens Reality, unable to account for the bountiful Reality of Holy Mystery; without science, spirituality thins out into naïve spiritualism, a magical thinking divorced from the dynamic laws of nature. Together, spirituality and science can open our consciousness to the surprising ways Spirit manifests in this time of COVID.

GRATEFUL (EUCHARISTIC) CREATURES

It is Moses—representing humanity's spiritual awakening—who begins to realize that the name of Reality he has been encountering is *I am who I am* (Exod 3:14). Moses and the Israelites, and through them the people of the West, are initially discovering the truth that Being is of the Reality we call Holy Mystery. Everything that arises into form is Being expressing, which is to say, Holy Mystery manifesting here and now. *God* is not a thing, or a law, or a ritual, but manifests simply as *I am*, which means the Mystery of Being. Moses and the people are afraid that as they continue their journey, they will be alone. But Moses, listening to the voice of his heart (which is humanity's heart), realizes that the Mystery of *I am who I am* will be with them—is with them—as Being, as Spirit, breathing as their being. So, they may be at rest.

Twenty-three hundred years later the Irish theologian and philosopher John Scotus Eriugena would, in his own way, deepen our understanding of Moses's realization. Holy Mystery is our true nature, in that it is as Being expressing that we exist as human creatures. Our body is from dust, but even this dust is not absent of Being. The twentieth-century German Jesuit theologian Karl Rahner further deepened the implications, enabling us to speak of creation itself as the *Ursakrament*, which simply means the *fundamental* sacrament. Why? Because creation, simply as it is, only exists

Grateful and Communal Creatures

because Holy Mystery is its true nature. Nature is and always has been *supernatural*, or a graced Reality arising from the Silence. Creation—as *Homo sapiens*, as mammals, as animals, and as all flora and fauna—is the beautiful face of Being. Holy Mystery is the Source of *all* that is. Spiritually, the evolving cosmos is telling the sacramental story of the gracious unfoldment of creation. Creation is the ebullient manifestation of the silent and empty Deep.

Albert Einstein's scientific theory of relativity, so elegantly and simply expressed in $E=mc^2$, enriched our appreciation further. What appears solid and inert to our senses is energy, dynamic and fluid. All that is, regardless of its form, is, spiritually speaking, a manifestation of form from emptiness, the singing of word from silence—emptiness and form, absence and presence, unmanifest and manifest, silence and word, nonbeing and being. All is Holy Mystery. There are no exceptions: from comets to computers, from insects to internet.

Since everything is a manifestation, a bodying forth, of Holy Mystery, the cosmos—known in the Christian story as the Body of Christ—is sheer gift (which is sacrament) as the womb of unfolding life. Each creature is Christ by nature and called to awaken as Christ heart, as it lives into and slowly realizes the truth of its Reality.

As we gaze up into the night sky or into the endless depths of our lover or at the resplendent, shimmering beauty of a sea anemone, how then do we receive what and who we behold? Our Christ heart—honest and vulnerable as an open womb—receives the beauty with grateful thanksgiving (which is to say, *eucharistically*). We are awed and humbled beyond words that this cosmos is the intimate bodying forth of Holy Mystery. When we grow callous or forgetful, our Christ heart longs once again, as Rumi so tenderly says, for the moon to press its face against ours and remind us of this tender and tenacious truth of who and what we are.[1]

Spiritually, to the degree we are awake to Reality as the Body of Christ, we are grateful, which is to say eucharistic creatures. The universe nourishes us without reserve and without thought because Spirit is effusive. The liturgical Eucharist (or Lord's Supper or Mass) is not a magical exception to life within a barren and inert universe, but rather is an embodiment, an expression in, of, and through which we recognize and celebrate that Holy Mystery *is* the Reality of creation, and we are humans *of* Being, awakening *as* Holy Mystery. To be human is to be a *eucharistic* being.

---

1. Rumi, "There Is Some Kiss We Want."

PART THREE: WORSHIP AS SUPPORT

COMMUNAL CREATURES

Being bodies forth as dynamic and evolving energy. Reality, never stagnant, is continually changing in its myriad modes of manifesting. No particular manifestation is ever without Holy Mystery as its true nature, even when distorted and destructive. To draw upon Paul, there is no "height, nor depth, nor any other created thing" (Rom 8:39) that can separate us from Holy Mystery—from the love which is God manifest as Christ heart. The life of Jesus clarifies for us that the nature of Holy Mystery is boundless love even in the cold, dark, vacuum of interstellar space or interpersonal relationships.

As our species evolves and our consciousness matures, new circumstances give rise to new modalities not experienced previously. In the wake of COVID, so-called virtual reality has become one of these relatively new modes of manifestation. Leaders and members of religious traditions, for whom the practice of communal Eucharist has been integral to their spirituality, often lament the supposed doctrinal fact that Communion is not possible because we can no longer be present together. All we have is the virtual gathering, utilizing *virtual* as a synonym for *not real*.

That is neither my experience nor understanding. Over many years of being with people on Skype and Zoom, there is clearly a sense of the presence of Holy Mystery when we are consciously present with one another. This created thing of the internet is not a solid wall inhibiting real presence but a new threshold to navigate. Holy Mystery is creatively manifesting itself in a mode that is novel and must be learned through experience. Too often prejudicial doctrine prevents us from listening to and learning from what our own heart and body are revealing to us. I continually encounter via Zoom participants feeding and really being fed by one another, as they learn to become attuned to the presence of Holy Mystery manifesting here and now in a new way.

THE DYNAMIC REALITY OF HOLY MYSTERY

Virtual is not simply a misnomer when it comes to accurately describing being with one another via a new modality, it is deeply mistaken about the very nature of Reality. When we are consciously present with one another, whatever the modality, we are Really with one another. There is nothing unreal about the experience. The modality, such as the internet, significantly shapes the experience. That is true. And we must learn to discern anew the presence of Holy Mystery within this new form, *how* we are present as Spirit adapts with the circumstances—but that is always the case. Each modality of the presence of Holy Mystery represents its own challenges for us. However, as humans of Being, our heart, mind, and body are always already in union with one another (communion). Our task is to discover how that is happening in this new modality.

Gaze gratefully up into the heavens above or deep within the one lying beside you. Share a congregational meal or Eucharist via Zoom, or coffee for two within a six-foot arc of loving-kindness. As humans awakening as Holy Mystery, we are eucharistic by nature and communion is our relational Reality. The grace within COVID is the discovery of learning to respond and be attuned to the circumstances that the dynamic Reality of Holy Mystery offers. We are gratefully learning to participate in real communion in a new modality. Our maturation lies in our practice of sensing into this new modality of awakening as Holy Mystery and discovering how to embody its vitality.

PART THREE: WORSHIP AS SUPPORT

EXPLORATIONS

1. As you gaze up into the night sky or into the endless depths of your lover or at the resplendent, shimmering beauty of a sea anemone, how do you receive what and who you behold? How do you experience your Christ heart? Remember, there is no right or wrong answer. You simply want to know the truth of your experience. Does grateful thanksgiving arise? How? Be specific as you can. Perhaps there is resentment? If so, how does that feel? Is it possible to be grateful (eucharistic) for whatever arises, seeing within it an invitation to explore and grow?

2. The liturgical Eucharist is not a magical exception to life within a barren and inert universe, but an embodiment, an expression in, of, and through which we recognize and celebrate that Holy Mystery is the Reality of creation, and we are humans of Being, awakening as Holy Mystery. What does it mean for you to recognize yourself as a eucharistic being?

3. When we are consciously present with one another, whatever the modality, we are really with one another. There is nothing unreal about the experience. The modality, such as the internet, significantly shapes the experience. That is true. And we must learn to discern anew the presence of Holy Mystery within this new form. How have you experienced being with others in communal liturgy via Zoom? What have been some of its challenges? What have been some of its surprises? Have you been aware of a field of presence in which all are present? What are some of the qualities you feel or sense in this field of presence? Can you feel such qualities as sadness, joy, intimacy? If so, how do they feel like and/or different from such qualities when you are physically with others? How might a communal liturgy via Zoom be strengthened?

CODA

Participating in the Song of Life

> After days of labor,
> mute in my consternations,
> I hear my song at last,
> and I sing it. As we sing,
> the day turns, the trees move.
>
> WENDELL BERRY, "I GO AMONG TREES AND SIT STILL," IN *SABBATHS*

BEGINNINGS ARE IMPORTANT. THE first lines of John's Gospel proclaim that "in the beginning was the Word" and "all things came into being through [the Word]" (John 1:1, 3).

We can hear these words literally as an historical assertion claiming that at some distant point in ancient times—the initiation of time—the Word (whatever that might mean) came into being as a kind of medium through which all else that has come to be was created. My sense is that this misses the poetic thrust of the mystical writer. Rather, I understand John to have experienced this not only in the beginning of each experience we have, but in the middle and culmination as well; there is this mystery he realizes is *the Word*.

But for most of us, most of the time, the beginning, middle, and end of our experience is not perceived as the Word (again, whatever that might mean). Rather, most of our experiences are generated by, sustained by, and understood in terms of unconscious fear.

Fear cannot only paralyze; fear can thrust us into fight or spur us into a hasty retreat. Peter Levine, in his seminal book on trauma *In An Unspoken Voice: How the Body Releases Trauma and Restores Goodness*, offers a testament in part to the power of fear to compel and compromise us, body and soul.

When some animals are threatened with death by a predator, such as an opossum, we commonly describe their paralyzed reaction as *playing dead*. But there is no play involved here at all. The overwhelmed nervous system is thrown into a last resort for survival, and all but shallow breathing shuts down as the brain stem takes control. Sometimes it works, and the predator loses interest. Sometimes it fails, and the opossum is some other creature's meal.

More often, the last-ditch survival mechanism of paralysis is not necessary. Rather, as the large and swift savannah cat attacks its prey, the hearts of the antelope accelerate their beat, sweat pours forth, breathing becomes rapid, pupils dilate, and the animals instinctively run or actively defend.

As humans, when our nervous system becomes overwhelmed, we can become catatonic. We don't choose to become immobile. Rather, our system shuts down as a final effort to survive. As with our evolutionary relatives existing on the Serengeti, ordinarily such extreme reaction isn't necessary. But all too often we experience our interactions of day-to-day life as if we were still striving to survive in the wild; at least that is how the experiences register in our nervous system. We have an interaction with our boss; we have an argument with our spouse; our daughter fails to arrive at home with the family car by 11 p.m. and now it is 2 a.m.; our parent is suffering from dementia. More often than not, before we are even aware, our heart has quickened, our breathing stopped or accelerated, we sweat, our head aches, and we are primed to flee or quarrel.

We feel compelled to at least do something to change what we currently experience as untenable. Fear, whether manifesting as flight or fight, expresses itself in and through the compulsion to do something to change what is. Ironically, we would rather die than not do, because we experience our non-doing as a kind of death by being overwhelmed by life.

And so, fear compels us to find something we can do to change the circumstances we experience as too much to handle. We don't know how to receive what life is presenting us. To take this one step further, fear, which surrounds and imbues our experience, has us convinced that Holy Mystery is not present in our frightening condition. We feel compelled to act in some way to get to a place where we hope the Beloved will be present. If the Beloved were present, fear-controlled reason concludes, then we would be able to rest and let be where we are.

To begin to get a sense of how pervasive fear is in Western culture, we need to recognize how thoroughly we have become a society of doers. We are utterly convinced that through doing we will be saved. As I said, we would rather die than not do. To fail to do—and to not do does register in our being as failure—is to leave us in the seemingly intolerable position of vulnerability and at the apparent whim of a capricious universe.

Even more, in our fear, which compels us to be a being who tries to control life, we reduce Holy Mystery, the Beloved, into a divine doer; just like us, only much bigger and much stronger and invulnerable.

All of which brings us back to the reforming experience and spiritual insight of the community in which the Gospel of John was written. This vulnerable group, feeling besieged in a turn-of-the-century culture whose seams are somewhat frayed, somehow realizes that before fear, and more profound and powerful than fear, is their experience of the Word, holding (as in an embrace) everything they are undergoing: threat from imperial Rome, discord with the Jewish synagogue, tense relations with other fledgling communities of the early Christ movement.

But what is meant by *the Word*? We hear that phrase, and it sounds like some thing. In the beginning was some thing, some object, called the Word. This is an instance where way too much is lost in translation. The Hebrew *dabar* and the Greek *logos* connote, not some thing, but a dynamic and vibrant *mystery*. We would do much better to say that in the beginning was *wording*. But that is awkward English and still misses the mark. We draw closer by saying in the beginning was *speaking*. Using the gerund, which is both noun and verb, helps us approach what John's community was awakening to in its heart—a dynamic presence in their life, always there. We can draw even closer to the true nature of this dynamic by expressing the realization poetically: in the beginning there was singing arising from the silent, absolute Deep. When the infinite depth of Holy Mystery expresses, what arises is song.

Part Three: Worship as Support

Life, John's Gospel is proclaiming, is a singing forth into life. If you consider a note of music, we can perceive it as an inanimate mark of notation on a page. But as physics reminds us, any thing we observe can be appreciated as a particle and as a wave—so, too, a note of singing. Each note of life is a divine wave of Spirit emanating from the infinite depth of Holy Mystery. We, each and every creature, are fluid notes of vibrant music. Creation itself is a symphony spontaneously composing as it manifests moment to moment from and as Holy Mystery.

(Take a moment or two now—maybe several moments—to hear the song of life emanating from your being. Hearing and sensing—or feeling—are so closely related. Sound is waves of air landing upon our eardrum. When we sense into our body—all of it, from toes to head, from back to front, from side to side—we can feel waves of life. The waves may be slight, or we may find our whole body swaying to music we hadn't known to be present. Every mood we feel is a movement waiting to be discovered and known, intimately—and with some joy.)

The intimate quality of this music invites us to experience this singing, so loving and so tender in its true nature, as divine cooing—like a mother humming softly and sweetly to her infant. Neither is really doing anything. They are not doers. They are fluidly participating in one another's being as the song that is their common Christ heart resonates throughout their bodies. They are embodiments of the infinite intimacy of Holy Mystery.

The opening words of John's Gospel are an invitation to grow into the wisdom of joyfully participating in life as song. Each creature that exists is a pulsating note; all things come into being as a wave of Holy Mystery manifesting in unique sonorous beauty. We never know what movement will arise on the breath of the next intonation—the tragedy of Mozart, the joy of Beethoven, the mourning and loss of Fitzgerald, the playful love of Ellington. Maybe a simple coo. We have no control over life's spontaneous unfoldment. But however Holy Mystery manifests, the breath of each note is a wave of boundless love; the presence within each note is always a tenor of undying compassion that holds even our fear. The invitation we receive, regardless of the movement of the song, is to learn to participate in, is to learn how to sing, the irreplaceably unique Christ heart song that is us.

PART FOUR

— Prayers & Psalms to Nurture —

How do you rise in the morning from the dark sea of sleep? I find that our perseverating mind commences before even drawing our fifth breath. With a bullet train of thoughts underway our nervous system is stimulated and sometimes already pumping our body with cortisol. Before we have even been able to land our feet on the floor, stress has been given new life at the break of day.

If we are to care wisely for our maturing soul and serve this world well, ask yourself how you might best arise so that you feel grounded, providing gracious space for your soul to awaken in the Reality of the moment. This is a rising which nurtures a relaxed belly, a soft heart, and an open and curious mind. This is your heart listening to the silence of the heart of the Beloved. The Christian monastic tradition starts the day with prayers called Matins. Our Matins is quite simple.

As we shake off the morning cobwebs, savoring our coffee or tea, receive the light that massages the darkness into the waiting ground, and sense into your awakening soulbody. You may notice that once again the mind easily begins to absorb our attention with its daydreaming and planning. Rather than being pulled along, we can settle into our soul's awakening with a gentle and focused prayer: Matins. As you pray each line, let the words guide your living response in the moment. For example, when you say, either silently or aloud, "Listening, I hear," attend to what you hear. Not with labelling the sounds, but with appreciation for each distinct sound gracing your soul. Your soul is being serenaded awake by the chorus of creation.

Speak slowly, with awareness, allowing time for your body to become alive in the moment in and through inhabiting Reality as invoked by the words. Allow space around each word and phrase so that their power for invoking presence might land within you. Let each become a wise container of your soul being quickened into the miracle of life this moment.

> As I arise today
> Listening, I hear
> Looking, I see
> Tasting, I savor
> Sensing, I awaken
> Conscious, I'm aware
> Grateful for the breath of life
> Living, I love
> Alaha, my home; my soul, your dwelling.

When I was in seminary in the early 1990s I was fortunate to be a student and later a friend of the marvelous liturgist Louis Weil. In one class, Louis invited each of us to create what today I would describe as a liturgical body prayer. That is, a somatic expression of the heart's communication with God. The "Abwun Gesture of Oneness," which can be prayed as either an early morning prayer or interchanged with the prayer of arising and so become another expression of Matins, is based upon the body prayer that arose in my soul as my heart communicated with my love. (Instead of words, we attend to the presence itself of Holy Mystery in and as our quickening soulbody. Facing east, if possible, we awaken along with creation, stirred by the dawn into movement out of the land of dark dreams.) Decades later I would discover its essential similarity to the salutation gesture that begins Diamond Body Practice developed by Linda Krier.

What I did not have present in my awareness in the 1990s was the essential role and power of sound as we pray and move. As the breath is shaped by vowels and consonants, it resonates uniquely in different areas of the soulbody, especially the head, heart, and belly. Many traditions make use of sound in prayer, including the Christian traditional singing of Gregorian Chant and Taizé. I draw upon the Aramaic word *abwun* (a-bw-oo-n), which is usually translated *father* and is the opening word in what is known as the Lord's Prayer.

Neil Douglas-Klotz clarifies for us that a more accurate translation of abwun would be something like *parenting*. "Abwun is the divine source continually parenting or birthing all appearance of form in a mysterious way, giving birth to something new this moment: my life."[1] In the "Gesture

---

1. Douglas-Klotz, *Revelations of the Aramaic Jesus*, 30.

of Oneness," the primary gestures of the body prayer are expressions of the breath as we speak the word *abwun* phonetically: ah—bwoo—n.

Ah, sounded with the mouth relaxed and open, resonates in the belly while the hands are before the head, integrating mind with body. As the hands move downward to the heart and point out horizontally, we sound *bwoo* through lips pursed as if blowing through a straw, with the focus on *oo*. Now the breath resonates in the heart and belly, integrating these two centers of the body. The hands then drop to the belly and point to the grounding earth as the breath sounds the *n*. The tongue lightly touches the back of the upper front teeth, leading to resonance of the breath in the head while the hands are at the belly. In this completion of the body prayer the mind resonates gently as it comes to rest in the ground of the body.

ABWUN GESTURE OF ONENESS

Stand with feet about shoulder-width apart. Eyes open with soft focus, looking straight ahead. Let arms and hands hang loose by sides, shoulders relaxed. Bend knees slightly as you inhale and raise arms outward in a gentle arc carrying the earth up to the heavens. Hands meet overhead, pointing upward to heaven as we breath ah, *pause, then slowly descend, bringing the heavens into the heart and resting in the body. When the hands reach the heart, they point horizontally embracing all that is, sounding the* bwoo; *bow slightly in reverence and gratefulness to Holy Mystery, concluding with the hands at the belly and pointing to the earth, the breath resonating with* n.

Once you have finished your coffee and breakfast, it is time to place the soulbody in the receiving presence of Holy Mystery. As with "Abwun Gesture of Oneness," the words for the "Abiding Liturgy for Morning" are few. The opening devotion and the closing dedication gracefully hold us as we practice sitting in meditation. We are awakening, moment by moment, day by day, realizing our Christ heart flowing into a life of service. If you can, sit with a friend, in person or via Zoom. But sit. Kindly allow yourself to be with yourself in silence, stillness, and solitude. The land of your soul is eternal and abundant in its very emptiness.

ABIDING LITURGY FOR MORNING

(Seated)

Part Four: Prayers & Psalms to Nurture

Devotion

> Beloved,
> You are the deep and the shallow.
> You are the fertile as well as the fallow.
> You are the honey and the bitter.
> You are the fire as well as the winter.
> You are the center without any edge.
> You are I am, and I am, too.
> I am your being.
> My soul lives as you.

Meditation (20–40 minutes)

Dedication

> As Holy Mystery,
> love through and through,
> I awaken and serve.

PRAYERS & PSALMS

Finally, we need prayers to nurture us along our journey, soulful reflections for each week of the year. Prayer is the heart's language of love with its Beloved. Here are the soul's musings, cries, bewilderments, longings, wonderments, songs, pleas, and so much more. These prayers and psalms collect the focus of the soul and invite you to sit with, explore, cry with, feel gratitude for the gift of boundless love that is Holy Mystery. They do not offer answers. They are conversation starters for your spiritual journey. They express the soul's longing to know the kiss of grace in every nook and cranny of her daily life. You might find it helpful to frame your reading, conversation, and inquiries of parts 1 and 2 with these weekly reflections. A key to spiritual practice is to root your reading in your present experience so that the knowledge you realize arises from and is validated by your experience. Feel free to draw on these as they resonate with your experience or allow yourself to be invited into the mystery of being surprised each week.

A JAGGED FRACTION

In our confusion
    we fear we will always be a jagged fraction,
never a resting whole;
        we feel a sunken captive to heavy shadows of anxiety;
            we mistake our
    lost and
            angry
    hearts
with Reality. The Beloved has become a cruel memory.

Awakening is the slow lifting from our soulbody
    of the weighted veil of ignorance.
Awakening is knowing that today is one of promise—
    not of more self-critical judgment
        but of surprising self-kindness.
Awakening is a soulful touch of tenderness
    that does not bruise
        but is a kiss of healing.
    This is the ancient marrow of truth of that word *salvation*.
Perhaps the edge of a smile within our longing soul.

YOUR BREATH ALONE

Flaming breath of the Beloved,
kindly burn away the chaff of restless thoughts and fearful passions, that
our brow uncreases,
our shoulders hang freely as willow branches,
our mouth smiles softly,
our heart beats gently,
our belly ebbs and flows like the evening tide,
and our body becomes the evening earth at rest.
Root our life,
stem, branch, and trunk,
in the fertile ground of abiding compassion.
Deeply nourish our soul, so that
from your breath alone (which is our own ruha,[1] however slight or strong)
we drink the Spirit of wisdom and understanding—

    this breath—*now*—is a gift that neither demands nor forces its way into
our body;
from your breath alone
we drink the Spirit of counsel and strength—

    this breath—again *now*—teaches us trust by discovering strength in
receiving;
from your breath alone
we drink the Spirit of knowledge and reverence—

---

    1. *Ruha* is Aramaic for the dynamic reality of breath, which Douglas-Klotz describes this way: Ruha is "a breath flowing freely, always connected with the source of Reality, *Alaha* (*Elohim* in Biblical Hebrew, *Allah* in Arabic). This breath continues without interruption beyond time and space, including when we are asleep. The sounds of RU ('roo') are open, felt in the chest and belly, without any sharp border." *Revelations of the Aramaic Jesus*, 18. He continues later: "As long as we have physical bodies, we hold on to the physical breath for life; yet there is a breath inside that breath which, from the viewpoint of Yeshua's [Jesus's] Aramaic, connects to soul, *ruha*. This *ruha*-breath is the activity in us that is always connected to Reality." 49.

this breath—again only *now* do we breathe—is simple, complete, a grace.

THROUGH YOUR LAVISH HEART

Beloved,
through your lavish heart runs the sacred path of unfolding life.
Open my eyes to behold your beauty in faces I do not understand.
Unstop my ears to receive your voice in music I would judge as strange.
Loose my tongue to sing your joy as I receive each moment.
Mend my broken body to flow as a dance to your song however I move.
So that as Christ heart,
I realize I am—as I am—the path of life,
this very day,
to all I meet.

TIMELESS WOMB

Luminous emptiness—
timeless womb
birthing
quark and quasar,
rose and redwood,
beetle and baboon,
wasp and whale,
Homo floresiensis and *Homo sapiens*;
you are Silence—
eternal Source
of every word arising from the deep.
I am your dark, rich, soil
tilled by ebb and flow of love
ripening through birth
as your soul.

THE GIFT ARRIVES

Sitting,
waiting,
watching,
as we lean forward
within the winter realm of darkness,
our body senses,
infused by the longing of our heart,
that this particular moment
holds promise.
The gift arrives when our eyes are open,
relaxed and no longer fixed searchingly on the horizon,
but seeing fully from an embracing periphery.
The voices of the night
fill our listening ears as a silent chorus
heralding a momentous event.
Our mind lies calm beneath the guardian stars
as our being
is now attuned only to the vibrant presence
throughout the body and expanding into the universe
of her arising soul.
No longer waiting, watching, or leaning,
we are a
luminous night soulbody,
pulsating as the Holy Source,
radiating a joy we believed impossible.

BELOVED RADIANCE

What is my light
for this journey for which there is no map?
A North Star
warmly radiating from my heart's core.
A luminous Mystery
known in each unknown step.
An unhidden Holiness
present in every ordinary kindness.
A beloved radiance—
    steadying strength of my uncertain and searching heart;
    settling presence of my ruminating and restless mind;
    softening relaxation of my armored body.
What is my light?
      My soul,
      awakening as
      the way, the truth, and the life,
      that is simple Christ heart.

CRIMSON WAVES

The love of Holy Mystery
cascades over creation,
thoroughly immersing us
in these fiery waters of consciousness
that slowly burn off the chaff of
lonely fear separating our soul from others, and
isolating ignorance that leads our mind to belittle creatures as cheap ornaments.
Renewed and refreshed by
life's crimson waves
the wings of our heart unfurl,
soft and moist,
and the gates of our mind lie open
with nothing to guard.
We enjoy—no, we relish—discovering
how to ride freely upon the waves of trust and curiosity
smitten by life's beauty.

SAVOR AS SACRED

Holy Mystery,
may we hold in trust
    the questioning mind,
    the searching heart,
    the restless body,
    and the thirsting soul.
May silence be the source of sound,
darkness be the deep of light,
aloneness be the awakening of intimacy.
May we savor as sacred
the many different paths of awakening as you.

BRILLIANT JEWEL

My Love
shines brilliant as a diamond from within the deep shadows.
My Love's light
is strong, steady, and sure, and strengthens my heart
for the journey beyond the familiar Jordan
to the land of my soul on the distant shore.
My Love's light carries my soul
    beyond the shadow of anger
    beyond the shadow of judgment
    beyond the shadow of rejection.
Even beyond the shadow of hungering to belong.
My Love's light touch
moment by moment tenderly and patiently
softens my being into a sweet citadel of Christic care,
a brilliant jewel of infinite kindness.

CLIMBING

There are those days—perhaps it is this day—
our exhausted heart pleads,
brought to our buckling knees
on life's mountain—
we can ascend no further.
We seek a face, familiar and kind.
We stand again. Why? We are not sure.
Our heart longs to touch her truth
through and through
with no remainder.
We climb and climb and climb and climb,
dropping deeper down with each step
further into the foundation of our soul.
    I Am mountain.
    I Am climb.
    I Am exhaustion.
    I Am rock, sky, dirt, fire, rain, wind.
    I Am pounding heart, racing mind, aching bones.
    I Am everything.
Then—

No more mountain.
No battle. No struggle.
No movement.
No thing. No I.
Am
Free.

HOME WITHOUT WALLS

I seek to be seen
by gentle eyes bathing my soul in kindness.
I wish to be welcomed
by a loving presence that is no stranger, and even dearer than a lover—
    my soul inviting my heart home.
These soulful yearnings
are my heart's warm muscle tissue awakening to life,
stretching and slowly quickening into being after a dormancy that has felt like death.
Death is no longer mistaken as life.
As seasons pass my heart unfolds as a home without walls,
or ceiling, or even floor.
An endlessly open chamber that is Rumi's guest house to all.
I still find my soul stretching and afterward feel a little sore,
and so is the way of awakening. Soreness is ok.
Home is beautiful.

A RESOLUTE LOVER

For far too long our heart has been
fearfully and fitfully tethered to threatening commandments
fed into our soul by authorities since we were small children.
For far too long our mind has been
frozen to conventional obedience dreading the curse of condemnation
told in stories assured to us as sacred.
But the Beloved's voice is whispering this very moment
within the chambers of our heart;
a resolute lover calling again and again and again;
she will not be twisted by ignorance into the distorted voice of human judgment,
nor will she be drowned by the din of religious chatter
and forgotten as silence.
Her whisper is our heart's own voice:
I am yours. You are mine. We are.
I am yours. You are mine. We are.

CRACKS AND CREVICES

I awoke this morning to discover that
your presence so permeates unfolding creation that
I now see perfection
even in the very cracks and crevices of this shattered world.
I feel an unbinding from the judgments that gnarl and harden my body:
    I'm learning a perfection
        in the emptying of my heart of hatred for those who have hurt me.
    I'm learning a perfection
        in the freeing of my mind from continual judgment of those I do
not understand.
    I'm learning a perfection
        in the delicate vulnerability of a body laid open,
        arms spread wide,
        and heart softened by tears of sorrow and gratefulness that
        feed my soul this very
        moment.

GENTLE SMILE

I am astonished
at how quickly, upon awakening,
    as if a thief has stolen into the recesses of my being before having
    sat on bed's edge,
my mind has become congested thick with worry.
Anxious before my fifth breath,
a prisoner of my own plans,
running down roads that end in a maze of darkness.
It is time to breathe, one precious breath at a time.
One   precious   breath   at   a   time.
I move my attention—and yes, I call upon my will—
    my faithful aide-de-camp that strengthens and supports my longing.
I feel my belly and being rise and fall with the ruha of Alaha.
Rising and falling slowly—but what is time when I'm being resurrected?
I come to myself in this morning moment,
arising as the clear and full moon,
feeling my Beloved's golden face against mine once more,
claiming my heart as her lover.
Now,
my heart,
a gentle smile.

CAVERNOUS DEEP

Holy, Holy, Holy.[1]
I will hear this widowed refrain
arise unbidden in the corner of a day
as it futilely tries to corral my soul's gaze upward
from whence my help shall come[2]—supposedly.
My heart does not follow; not from being resistant.
The refrain rings hollow within my being.
My Beloved is unfathomable and eternal,
a sweet truth surrendered to me by a lover after many a midnight tête-à-tête.
Not from above, but from the cavernous deep,
the soulful cry of love rises and captures me:
    Come, pull out and away from the safe shore
    to which you cling so desperately.
        Leave your home of familiar refrains—it is empty.
        Desert your city of childhood fears—its promises waste your time.
        Let go of false treasures that sparkle but don't shine—they only
enslave.
    Let go and let your heart
    drop deep, deep—endlessly deep,
    into the emptiness that is Christ.
Here,
rich and dark
is the fullness of unbridled love.
Holy, Holy, Holy.

---

1. Isa 6:3.
2. Ps 121:1.

NOTHING ROTE

Such a foreign symbol in this strange land of ours,
a cross of ashes staring blankly from a forehead.
Words rotely spoken,
remember, *you are dust and to dust you will return.*[1]
A ritual over and done.
Nothing could be further from truth.
What a gift, 13.8 billion years in the making,
standing here as conscious carbon beyond all evolutionary odds.
Beautiful dust we are,
coalesced into existence through love.
The cosmos inexorably slows and cools,
yet quickened and warm
here we are.
There is nothing rote about you and me.
Chance. Yes. Grace. Oh, yes.
Holy Mystery is all inclusive.
Boundless love is the gloriously inglorious womb of this cosmic dust
each creature is and no one escapes.
No curse. Reality.
The Beloved is the pulsing heart of every moment of the billions unfolding.
This day calls us to attend to the fragility, the preciousness, of us, of life.
Nothing rote. A soul's plea:
Beloved,
present within,
be a fire consuming my heart:
    burn away shame that imprisons my soul;
    burn away rage that drives me to vengeance;
    burn away fear that dwindles me down to despair of your love.
Leave nothing buried in these ashes,
but a grateful Christ heart.

1. Gen 3:19.

I, TOO, LONG

An odd feast to celebrate in the twenty-first century:
a first-century Jewish rabbi riding into a Middle Eastern town upon an ass.[1]
A Don Quixote tilting hopelessly at Roman windmills?
Not really.

A human being no longer controlled by conventional norms,
nor caged by fear of failure in the eyes of others.
A human being who can't be missed but doesn't need to be noticed.
A human being fully content with himself,
no longer hungry for approval or acceptance,
but living directly from the wisdom of being love unbound.

I, too, long to no longer be weighed down
by small, controlling notions of right and wrong;
I, too, long to no longer be buffeted about
by passing thoughts and fleeting emotions;
I, too, long to no longer be consumed
by vain pursuit of false gods to confirm self-worth.

I, too, long to know that
wisdom has built her home of my heart,
supple and strong and spontaneous;
solid as a mountain, fluid as a stream, clear as the sky, deep as the ocean:
> free to mount an ass, place a flower in the barrel of a tank,
>> exist decades under house arrest or live beside gorillas in the jungle,
> or be at home right here.

---

1. Matt 21:1–11; Mark 11:1–11; Luke 19:28–40; John 12:12–16.

SEA OF GENEROSITY

Life is a banquet
overflowing from our hearts
as they learn the dance of love.
We whirl and twirl and whirl and twirl
hearts bursting into flames
that reduce our sense of
    awkwardness and uncertainty, our
    fear of tripping and stumbling, our
    anxiety about what comes next or afterward,
to ash.
Christ heart alone remains,
and that is what we are.
Prodigal love pours forth
inviting all to the dance
opening out upon the sea of generosity.
Free,
we sea dancers,
supremely free:
in our stock,
in our branches
and all the fruits of our branches.
We are willows and cypress freely swaying,
as the sap of sweet, flowing wine flows, and
pulsates our being.

FRIENDS[1]

Fear, panic, betrayal, isolation, death.
These were the watchwords of Good Friday.
Sermons hammered home the lesson that
human beings were creatures who turn and fled and lied
when incomprehensible fear swallowed us whole.
But I have seen and known a different human heart.
I have felt the hand of my lover soft and resolute
as I received the worst of news.
I have sat anointed in a sea of loving tears shed by friends and family
amid body-numbing suffering.
These are companions,
steady and present when life shatters apart.
The women did not flee Jesus in panic.
They knew fear.
Absolutely.
I have no doubt.
They didn't deny or suppress,
but held that panic-ridden passion in their heart,
and let it rest in the larger world of their
love for their friend.
They were companions: that is the message of Good Friday.
In our loneliest hours,
when we cannot feel our limbs,
when our soul wants to contract to a leaden point in our head,
and our heart is hopelessly numb,
friends companion us through.
The women stayed with Jesus.
He was not abandoned. They did not run.

1. See Luke 23.

They loved and beheld and anointed with their tears.
Friends are the divine face of mercy,
the kindest presence,
of the One whom our soul loves,
and sometimes simply cannot find,
amid loss and death.

WASH OVER US

In water are we conceived.
In water are we knit together in ruha.
Through the breaking of water are we born.
Through the drinking of water are we nourished.
You, Alaha, are living water:
Still, Silent, Deep.
May you wash over us,
in and through every cell,
caressing every pore,
kissing kindly every dry bone and muscle,
until we trust again in our beauty,
and our hearts fall open
enamored by grace of creation.

CURIOUS WARRIOR-OF-THE-HEART

This is the day,
when you,
like curious Thomas from the Bible,[1]
are no longer satisfied
with secondhand knowledge
for what is true.
You need to know for yourself.
You need to plant your knees upon the earth,
turn over the dirt,
scratch through the leaves,
bloody your own hands,
shed your own precious tears.
You need to stick those bruised fingers into the side of life,
probe around a bit—maybe a hell of a lot.
You need to know for yourself,
what a wound, your wound, feels like from the inside.
Moist. Warm. Exquisitely sensitive.
No secondhand story,
nor word of mouth tidbit.
This is the moment you know,
whatever you know,
directly,
immediately,

---

1. Convention, influenced by the Gospel of John, burdens Thomas with the moniker of *doubting* (John 20:25). The Gospel of Thomas, replete with wisdom sayings from Jesus, and dated by many scholars as one of the earliest Gospels, paints a rather different picture. Thomas embodies the curiosity of early Christians whose faith was rooted in the trust of their experience, taught them by Jesus. Elaine Pagels, in *Beyond Belief*, "breathes new life into writings once thought heretical," enabling us to see a Thomas that inspires and grounds the life of faith.

for yourself.
You're courageously embarking on the path of flesh and faith,
learning to trust your own experience,
no longer settling for the meager droppings left by others
in their pronouncements of belief.
You are willing to fall fully into the deep of your humanity,
and learn to swim for yourself.
Let the doubts, the questions, the uncertainties, come full force.
You are a curious warrior-of-the-heart,
Christ heart,
who probes and searches and explores and wonders.

LOVE BENDS

He cried,
The arc of the moral universe is long, but it bends toward justice.[1]
Why?
Because that cosmic curvature
is the fluid fabric of love,
the substance of our soul and
the reality
of life-with-another.
How long is long?
That is hard to say.
I, for one,
am being constantly surprised
by how attached I am to the mosaic of blindness
birthed in my judgments.
Washing the scales from our eyes
can be scratchy, slow, uncomfortable
to say the least.
But this arc of divine love
coursing as the Being of creation
is patience beyond belief.
Love bends as a river runs,
carving its way through
rock, desert, forest, and field,
caressing into life
with the once-tears-of-the-sky.
A grace it is
this river that is life,

---

1. Quote attributed to Dr. Martin Luther King Jr. See Block, "Theodore Parker and the 'Moral Universe.'"

this fluid cosmic arc that flows and
never runs dry.
The bend
is this small moment
and every moment
of a line that is never straight but is
the moist curve of the arm of love
strengthening us for the journey,
supporting us
as the eyes of our heart
heal and open
beholding as Christ
those whose pains and sorrows
we touch this day.

MARROW OF DESIRE

Yesterday,
I arose as black emptiness,
in those thin hours before birds sing,
infinite deep dispelling the insistency of want and the persuasiveness of fear.
Not so the other day,
when the persistent power of their presence
was a weighty force almost beyond my reckoning.
I do not need a shepherd to
guide me around these ancient voices
abiding in my mind and body.
I do not need to be taught to whistle
as if the sounds arising from my bones
are to be avoided like a graveyard walk.
Today,
I feel the marrow of desire
coursing through the thrust of all my wanting.
I don't take the familiar bait,
nor do I act as if I have no hunger.
I do not whistle.
Let the voices have their say and stir my senses
in their habitual way.
As love,
I am learning to listen and let be.
Love is a powerful shepherd,
arising as the substance of my soul to behold as friend
what I have feared as slave master.
I do enjoy the freedom
to welcome within
whatever arises
this time.

GO OFF-ROAD

Happiness does not lie
nestled somewhere in the future.
Awakening is not becoming
someone other than our soul's true nature.
Realization is not getting
someplace else.

We don't trust
that we are enough.
It seems impossible and sounds ludicrous.
But that is the invitation of spiritual practice:
for the heart to discover that nothing is missing or amiss.
In this discovery lies our spiritual journey.
Every nook and cranny of our being
waits to be beheld worthy of being known, being touched, being listened to.
So often the elixir of awakening
is the tears of a grateful soul
appreciating with wonder
a shame-hardened corner of the heart.
Become an explorer
no longer confined by the comfortable corners of an inert map.
Go off-road into the hinterland of your soul.
You are discovering home.

SUNG INTO BEING

Before there is a before,
there is only
infinite dark and silence of womb.

Singing is the beginning—
gentle vibrations of air
caressing womb into birthing.

Silence sounds as song—
the cooing of womb's heart
the first movement into life.

A love song is the primal force
drawing forth womb into birthing.
No oxytocin required.

Boundless love,
somehow present not in dark silence,
but as dark silence of womb.

Boundless love present where nothing exists
but possibility of life
waiting for song's invitation.

You and I are not born of accident,
nor of plan.
We are being sung into being by love.

TINY TOUCHES

That warm face
bends down close to ours,
curves tenderly into a smile—
our heart knows you.

Lips resting on our ear,
soft sounds caressingly whispered
flowing down to our toes—
our heart knows you.

Moist breath
gently and sweetly filling
our tiny being with honey love—
our heart knows you.

We emerge together,
you and I,
as new beings in this world.
Sacred separate selves
weaving life through
tiny touches of tenderness.

PREGNANT ABSENCE

Abwun
caresses my being
in the pregnant absence of silence
as breath flows unwilled.
She is midwife,
massaging life from
fear-hardened heart.
She is wisdom,
palpably present
in the space of wordless moment.
I am dialogue
of love with
nothing spoken.

NOTHING IS EXTRANEOUS

I sat this morning,
mind chattering away;
choppy little waves on a shallow pond
continually stirred by winds of wanting.
Yet the deep remains,
upon which the seemingly shallow rests.
No pushing aside or judgment here,
but an allowing and a wondering:
soul's tender kiss
kindly embracing all that arises.
True holiness, this
self-kiss that draws forth and receives life
from what might first seem an intrusion, an obstacle.
I relish the grace of rest
born of awareness that
nothing is extraneous or excluded
in awakening as
Holy Mystery.

NO LONGER ADRIFT

Abwun,
    as we would drift into sleep while even awake,
    and would fall into dream with eyes wide open,
the engine of a passing car
is the unexpected gift
that lands upon our soul and
once again, we are here, now, in this moment.
This utterly ordinary moment,
extraordinarily brief,
known only because we are no longer adrift
in the dream of passing thoughts.
No moment is without a bell to stir the heart,
    whether it be a bird's call, a child laughing, a leaf's rustle.
Creation speaks,
the voice of love undeterred,
inviting us to hear and listen to
the sounding of deep unto deep.

WEIGHTLESS GRACE

I am surprised at the sheer leaden weight,
lifeless poundage—
pressing fast as the deadening force of judgment.
Self-criticism descends with
the universe's primal thrust of gravity,
relentlessly compressing our life,
squeezing out all the moisture of joy and laughter,
leaving disheartened shadow
that—only moments ago—was
flowing life graced with dreams and smiles.
More surprising still—
the reviving power of the
soft gaze of kindness that
warms and releases the soul,
landing with weightless grace,
like the rains of spring that water the earth.[1]
The gift of another's azure eyes, pools of blue,
are salty drops of life upon the cheek,
slowly coursing their way as rivers of kindness
throughout our fearful being,
caressing the desiccated heart into warm flesh again.
When judgment would abandon us like
Lazarus to the grave,[2]
these holy waters kindly seep into the cracks and crevasses
of our hardpan and we arise,
as the earth budding anew in the spring,
walking once again in the garden of our soul.

1. Hos 6:3.
2. John 11:1–44.

SEA OF GEMS

Deception narrows
the breadth of what the heart finds lovable.
In time we find ourself cherishing less and less,
fearful that generosity threatens diminishment of our self
and the fracture of our fragile sense of value.
We become accustomed to dwelling
in the small, small world
of the terrain of the all too familiar.
Tradition is reduced to what it is we like and
personal preference becomes our narrow holy grail to survival.

Such is the path of fear as it deceives the soul into fearing for her life.
There is no way around fear.
Nor can we destroy deception.
Ridicule is of no real use.
Nor is judgment of much help.

Kindness is found in clear compassion.
We have been deceiving ourself that we are
too small and too weak
to be with the world as it is.

But now we are learning to appreciate ourself
for who and what we truly are.
We are the body of Alaha,
beautiful and mighty and a pleasure to be and behold.

We look out upon a sea of gems,
holy beings learning how to live.

They are no threat.
They are precious companions.

The waters of Siloam wash away the cataracts of deception.[1]
No one, no thing, to fear;
an infinite invitation to learn to love
in this field of life.

---

1. John 9:1–11.

RECEIVING

Some evenings,
after a day that won't end,
when we feel like we have been flung by forces unknown
like Texas dust across an Oklahoma sky,
only to be plunged downward into depths heavy upon heavy—
on some such evenings as these,
if we pause, look, listen, and feel,
we might sense a gracious, singular, cool breeze upon our cheek, or
hear the peepers' small voices arising as hope with the new spring, or
look within to find our heart settling and slowing and longing.
These are signs that faith is present,
arising not as a thought
but as a slow sense of trust in this moment
that once seemed so utterly daunting.
We are discovering that the power of intimacy
is its transfiguration of fear.
We look and now see.
We listen and now hear.
We feel and now love
what is as it is, and
as it is it is so much more than what our fear believed.
We are not turning away. We are not turning.
We are receiving. That is what transfiguration is.
Receiving.

AUTUMN LEAVES

Longing
is a bridge for the heart,
carrying her over the emptiness
of separation and loneliness.
Longing
is the oxygen
sustaining the cry of the soul
for her abwun—behold me, all of me.
Longing,
relentlessly unrequited,
teaches us that there is
no thing out there, or, in here,
to fulfill us.
Longing
is the inexhaustible guide,
embodying the soul's awareness
that we are incomplete
only because we are
unaware of the truth of what we are:
Love, through and through.
We long until we rest in our own being
and we discover rest
only after all our longing lies spent as autumn leaves,
fertile ground of solitude.

BEHOLD

She solitarily pushes the remainders and reminders
of her life—
    four broken shopping carts of odds and ends brimming full
    that comprise her portable remnants of necessity
    and love—
up the hill beside the onlooking drivers on their way to work
near the woods
where I walk our dog—who sleeps quite well
with us.
There is no easy nor simple
answer,
let alone
the answer,
to this blatant and demeaning suffering.
But—
there is response.
No hiding. No dissembling.
A heart, a Christ heart,
able and willing
to care as well as is possible.
A heart working with others
who care.
The personal fibers of the
horizontal beam of the cross
extending as a lifeline of hope
to the Holy One before us who suffers.
The vertical beam of the cross—
    awakening as Holy Mystery—
a heart living fully and alertly
in this world

in all its complexity.
Awakening as Holy Mystery is
learning
to trust our capacity to respond
wisely
to what our heart,
our Christ heart,
beholds.
What do you behold this day?

SUPREMELY FREE

Abwun,
my prayer is not that you be
the sovereign of my heart.
Though I was taught those words
from the holy books themselves.
I do not seek a ruler or emperor or monarch
of my soul.
I seek the substance of my soul itself.
Is this substance some kind of treasure?
Yes, if truth be the holy grail.
My longing is to be the love that
I am,
and to live as that love that
I am.
This is love that
is free,
supremely free,
in root and branch.[1]

---

1. I draw upon the language of Porete, *Mirror of Simple Souls*, 160, when I speak of Christ being supremely free in root and branch.

WETLANDS OF MY HEART

I feel the weight of grief within my eyes as I awaken.
Before my toes can snuggle the carpet
I sense the tide of liquid sadness
pushing against the shores of my heart.
My chest is tight.

Grief is sadness joined with loss of what has been and might never be again.
My ego would prefer I push this discomfort to the side
and move forward,
as if it were a mirage created from the ether.
But grief is the face of love mourned,
reminding our soul
who we cherish matters.
We grieve because we love and love dearly.

Each simple step to my chair
honors my loss and
invites me to breathe into the sea of sadness.
I know I will not drown,
though this truth has taken years to penetrate my sinews.
Breathing is not a life buoy keeping me above the sadness.
Sitting,
I am dropping beneath the surface into the black sea of sorrow.
I settle. I feel. I continue to breath.

I discover my soul holding this sea without reserve.
Ah. My belly relaxing, I breathe more freely.
I had no idea how vast is the land of the soul
and how there is room for whatever arises
in the morning, in the evening, or in the dead of night.

These tears flowing from the wetlands of my heart
carry me to the surprising homeland of presence and stillness.
I slowly open my eyes as my wife leans in for a kiss.

DROP-DEAD GORGEOUS

For many years,
and length here is immaterial,
our soul fears being exposed
     as a fraud
     as incompetent
     as weak
     as mistaken
     as dumb
     as incompetent.
A guard dog stands ready at the gate of our heart
to keep others out, yes.
But even more,
to hold us back from letting ourself out.
No exposure—no judgment. That is our hope.
Safe and suffering as an unknown. That is our dream.

We need a wise teacher
who is a patient question.
No demands.
We need a guide whose love is a natural solvent
upon the frozen locks of our gated heart.
Never prying. Always wondering. Constantly present as kindness.
We need a companion
as the land of our soul breaks open
laying our most tender secrets beneath the open sky.

May you awaken through the birth pangs
of your questions.
May you emerge from
the holy womb of your wonderment

radiant with the joy
that you are drop-dead gorgeous,
from head to toe.

FRUIT IN SEASON

I have slowly realized that there is
no path into our heartland
other than through what the heart is giving us.
Wishing for another way through will not work.
Maybe you would prefer to feel clear today
but when you look closely,
the mind of your heart is a muddled mess.
Maybe your druthers are for feeling light and infused with joy,
but your limbs are heavy and cumbersome to bear.
There is no feeling within our heartland
that is not a fruit worthy of being tasted and savored.
I know this sounds ludicrous.
Who wants to taste and savor loneliness, or anger, or confusion?
But the heartland offers the only fruits that are in season at that moment.
No other fruits exist.
We can't pick and choose.
We can only learn to receive what is within.
> This fruit alone is the Beloved's offering to us.
> Prickly?
> Tough?
> Sweet or sour?
> Allow yourself the chance to be surprised.
> Within this fruit awaits the universe of love.

STARDUST DOMICILE

Wisdom
has built her house[1]
somewhere in our midst.
I have wondered where it is.
Some say it is the Scriptures.
Others lay claim to doctrine.
What about science?
I find glimpses of truth
in them all.
But as my soul seeks further,
I meet Wisdom
dwelling resplendent
as the ordinary creatures of creation.
Each being—
     a caterpillar, a chickadee, a dolphin, a Joshua tree—
is a ripening mystery.
Each is a budding question inviting wonder that
need never cease.
And what a marvel is
the house
of the inexhaustible human heart,
never a mere ho-hum dwelling,
but a vibrant, one-of-a-kind, stardust domicile
respiring with ruha.
Wisdom is domestic.
Her warm breath feeds our soul and her
soft light shines from within the
hearth of our heart,
illuminating the ground of our being
as simply holy.

    1. Prov 9:1.

CANAL OF LOVE

Alaha
is the divine womb
birthing each child
in a travail of blood, sweat, and tears;
the canal of love
issuing forth life,
precious and fragile,
beautiful and broken.
There is no alternate route.
Love is not a choice,
but cradling-Reality itself.
No hard edges in this womb
to cordon off unwanted bits or parts.

Evolving creation is awakening
through billions of years of travail.
The process has no end point.
The depth and breadth to the truth that Reality is
love through and through;
no corners, no edges, no finality.
Love is a mystery.
Everything ends, but love!
Moment to moment,
unshakable cradling love:
fathomless silent Source of
intimate tender mercy.

LISTEN CLOSELY

Have you ever felt betrayed
and discovered the overwhelming power
the searing wound can beget?
A relentless hunger for retribution
consumes the soul and sets the mind whirling with
interminable plans for exquisite vengeance.
Forgiveness hits our head like a lead-pipe dream.
Say goodbye to spiritual equanimity and peace.
Pain courses our veins like hot lava.
We pray, we pace, we plot, we futilely try to sit,
but scheme instead.
We can feel reduced to an unpredictable volcano—
no one knows when we will erupt.
And we can try so damned hard to be so good.
A voice from the far edge of the mind scolds,
You are better than this;
you are a spiritual being.

Listen closely, my friend;
let your heart rest gently upon mine.
Our hearts beat as one.
Receive me as your own breath.
Ah—there is soft space present you had not noticed.
Your mind is misleading you.
You think there is a gap between us,
a canyon created by what you have felt.
I am your soul calling you home—a womb of mercy.

WHERE ALL POSSIBILITIES BEGIN

I invite you to relax,
because the ordinary is where all possibilities begin.
We are spiritual wonderers,
because we know we have no idea what might be arising.

The womb of every word is Silence.
Every creature is born from Emptiness.
The Silence and Emptiness
gracefully arise in time and space as
you, me, and every creature.

A sacramental encounter begins with
beholding what is right there before us
in all its simple and straightforward beauty.
We don't need to add any adornments.
We don't need to subtract anything as extraneous.
Silence is speaking.
Emptiness has incredible form.

Awakening is realizing the infinite depth
within the sacred surface—it's all one boundless Reality.
We don't need to search for some extraordinary encounter.
Let the eyes of your soul *rest* upon the surface
where life continually bubbles up
and can so easily slip by unseen and unexplored
for what it truly is: Holy Mystery.

GENTLE CHAMBERS

Be thou my vision,
O Lord of my heart.[1]

Whatever befalls me,
be the *Heart of my heart.*

Be thou my vision,
that my ever-vigilant eyes
exhausted from standing sentry to my soul
may relax.

When I feel a rebuke, a mistake, a dismissal
as a hammer blow,
reverberating with ancient doubts about my worth,

Be thou my vision,
an Endless Ocean of Soothing Mercy.

Be thou my vision,
Heart of my heart,
whose gentle chambers
bathing all in kindness,
gently loosening the resentment
entangling my weary soul.

---

1. So sings the yearning, even pining, opening text of the traditional Irish ballad, translated by Mary E. Byrne.

PERSISTENT PILGRIMS

My day is closing and I wonder what was happening
as I resisted the generous impulses of my heart?
Maybe I didn't feel like being generous today; I was tired.
Maybe I didn't like this person before me; they grate my nerves.
Maybe I was dimly aware of a judgment that they don't deserve my generosity.
Maybe I felt I didn't know how to be generous today.
If I'm honest, I felt, *Why can't someone be generous to me? Isn't it my turn?*

Maybe, today, I just hated the whole notion of being generous so much
I wanted to collapse and cry, away from all eyes.
I was once told, *Never deny a generous impulse.*
I hear this as all air and no breath.
It lands upon my soul like countless other spiritual commands
sent from above to judge and override how I feel.
Better if we let the word die before it kills us with spiritual rigor mortis.

I wonder, why do we resist?
I invite you to learn the ways of your heart.
Isn't that an ironic invitation: be generous with your self? So be it.
Love is prodigal with you as you honor your confusion.
Let the tenacious tethers of judgment slip away from your soul.
Be surprised. Relish the release.

The Beloved invites us to become persistent pilgrims of the heart;
going beyond the judgmental forces that tug and tear at our soul.
We are crossing into the promised land of the heart's prodigal kindness,
where our soul is being lavishly bathed in kindness with each beat and breath.

RETURN AS A DWELLER

Turn inward to the land of the soul
and feel into the many chambers of your heart.
Your inner terrain may feel familiar or
maybe you've fallen into
an unrecognizable lunar landscape.
The voice of fear burying your will beneath a chorus of doubt,
calling you back to the confines of the mind.

How will you respond to the voice of fear and its chorus of doubts?
You may speak directly to the voice and say, *You are not true.*
You may take up your prayers.
You may try to drown the voice with song.

I suggest that you return again and again to the land of your soul.
Not a thought about your land, nor a memory.
Return as a dweller of your beating heartland.
If you must, begin over and over and over,
with breathing into your soulbody.
Learn to hear as you listen.
Learn to see as you look.
Learn to savor as you taste,
Learn to love as you feel.
Let your consciousness blossom into awareness,
your heart crying,
Beloved you are my home, and my soul, your dwelling.

PULSING PRESENCE

Abwun,
may your moist lips press against ours and breathe life,
quickening this earthen vessel of
    bone
    flesh
    heart
    mind
as your
pulsing presence,
generous kindness,
simple beauty.
Remind us this day,
lest we become lost amidst the movement and multitude,
to gently pause,
rest and breathe,   rest   and   breathe,   rest   and   breathe,
until once again
we live only as You.

AN UNDAUNTED COMPANY

I sat to sense my body this morning.
No rush; a sincere soul.
But I had fallen asleep
and felt nothing.
I was floundering in the subterranean channels of my mind:
heart panicking and butterflies flying.
The ground beneath my feet had dissolved.

I needed help.
I needed the wise compassion of my soul friends.

Awakening is not a solitary journey.
We are not isolated heroines and heroes conquering the ego.
We are members of an undaunted company,
all traversing the most challenging terrain of life.

Turn to your friends in time of need when you are suffering.
Spread open the wings of your trembling heart
and allow their presence to hold you
as you find the holy ground that never left
and unfolds again as the land of soul.

SELF-MERCY

Have you felt that trembling in your solar plexus,
    —that exquisite, fine, nexus of nerves receiving input from throughout your body—
energy stuck and vibrating beyond conscious control?

Have you sensed within to discover your belly churning,
and as you feel gently into that whirlpool
you become aware of fear rising upward through your chest,
heart beating fast and hard through bone and skin?

Love invites you to wonder about your experience,
holding your anxiety lightly as a precious threshold of mystery.

Courage is the heart discovering capacities she never believed possible,
such as holding fear, not at arm's length, but in cradling arms with wonderment.
Appreciating our fear without judgment.
Exploring our experience,
not as an intellectual problem to be solved or a failure to be remedied,
but as the soulbody speaking her heart and sharing her suffering.

May we receive fear as an invitation to learn self-mercy,
honoring our struggling being with kindness and openness and patience.
May we persevere as a river winding gently but surely to the sea.

WAVE RIDERS

Upon first opening my eyes
too early in dark of morning from troubled sleep,
I feel trapped by yesterday's debris on the bank,
and though surrounded by water,
bone-dry with loneliness.
The cool running stream doesn't even feel as close as a forgotten memory.
Vaguely aware of stumbling through the day,
I'm captured by the hunger of my eyes vigilant for rescue.

It isn't that we aren't trying.
Waking up is lifelong.
We are wrestling with shadows as we sleepwalk.
In our dream, we are forever stuck in the shore's muck.
Nothing is moving except our effort.

As the sun's sweet morning waves
carry away the dense droplets of sleep's fog,
our soul glimpses signs of a miracle:
all rivers do run to the sea.[1]
All. Not some.
This is our healing.

All rivers run to the sea
in which we already live.
The mind is stuck,
but life never ceases to move.
We are all flowing currents.
We don't need to swim harder or faster.

1. Eccl 1:7.

We need to discover how to float upon the current of life—
not as passive flotsam,
but as fluid wave riders.

Each feeling of captivity.
Each sense of being adrift.
Each fear of being lost.
All of it.
Indeed, every loss and longing
is of the wave we discover how to ride.
Nothing is jetsam.

Each experience we touch with awareness
carries us along in the sea.
We *are* water,
you and I,
always flowing,
a river of grace.

DANCING WITH ABANDON

Beloved
    of loss, as well as gift;
    of confusion, as well as clarity;
    of sorrow, as well as serenity;
    of absence, as well as touch;
    of tears, as well as laughter;
    of grief, as well as joy;
    of darkness, as well as dawn;
    of death, as well as birth.

You
are the Holy Source
holding as One
what our mind would
separate, judge, and discard.
Sometimes we are afraid,
shutting the door to protect our heart,
which feels small and vulnerable.

No one taught our soul to
hold gently, explore, let alone, befriend the darkness.
I don't mean as an act of piety or belief;
nor as trial sent from beyond to test us.

We thrive only if we test all the waters that ripple or rage
through our life.
If loss,
or confusion,
or grief,
or death,

be before us,
may we honor their presence,
even if it be with sadness and trepidation,
as we would clarity, serenity, birth.

We are here to learn the wisdom
of a heart with wings open wide,
of a mind free to test both edge and center,
of a body dancing with abandon,
of a soul with tears flowing and eyes glowing.

SILKEN SILENT VOICE

Buck and I
were slowly walking through our neighborhood
beneath an Oregon autumn azure heaven.
We both were smiling—his tongue hanging joyfully.

A slightly cool breeze tickled his nose and caressed my face.
The breath of the sky was whispering to my being,
kissing the eyes of my soul to open.
A silken, silent voice enfolded me
in an eternal embrace.
The persistent grief of my heart
was given a seat of repose.
Nothing need change.
Life is whole and utterly holy.

Have you heard this silent voice in the solitude of your soul?
You don't need to listen hard.
You do need to listen sincerely,
the ears of your heart soft.

For my part,
my grief had grown from an unplanned
visit to the Field Museum in Chicago
and the exhibit of *Evolving Planet*—
a stunning tour de force of evolution at play.
My being had sagged with heaviness.
The magnificent story was incomplete,
missing the internal dimension
of Alaha
within every molecule, cell, and creature

that exists and evolves in
the combustible symphony of unfolding life.

My prayer?
May we receive Love as endlessly inviting, ripening without even the capacity for control.
May we know Alaha as Holy consciousness birthing creation.
May we appreciate love as that mysterious power of life
    of prokaryotic and eukaryotic cells evolving over billions of years
    to the magnificent panoply of creatures today
    that includes you and me.
May we embrace our Mystery because our questions never end;
and the whole evolving panoply of life,
    earth, land, sky, water,
is Holy,
because all of it,
    massive extinctions and human cruelty,
    my dad's Parkinson's, the dead robin in the yard, my cancer,
is cradled in love that is never extinguished.

What might the blue sky and the cool autumn breeze
birth this day in your soul?

WITHOUT STINGY EDGES

The rains fall far and wide through the night,
full, heavy drops, landing with life on the roof,
running to and through the eaves,
tiny rivers slowly making their way back to the sea.

You and I are slowly making our way back to the sea;
a sea so wide that its waters are always already here.
There's a wideness in God's mercy,
like the wideness of the sea.[1]

No meanness or narrowness here.
Wideness without stingy edges.

Mercy is love softened further,
if that be possible,
by tears and touch of tender kindness anointing all suffering.

We can become quarry workers of the soul,
as if pounding stone with our fists
to destroy the barriers we believe
wall us off from the wideness of mercy's sea.

Rain falls, as does holy water, down our cheeks,
dissolving walls and
revealing to our soul
that we are no isolated island
but a soft, round, wide lake of love.

---

1. Faber, "There's a Wideness in God's Mercy."

Sense into your soul and
feel her strong and supple wideness.
The liquid land of our soul is
a boundless sea of merciful love.

HOLY SWEAT

Birthing life is bloody and messy.
Pushing, relaxing, crying.
Exhaustion.
Longing and fearing in the same breath.

Fortunately,
the midwife's skillful hands guide and support;
a heart teaming with wisdom,
steeped in life's womb.

It is easy to become confused,
captive to anxiety,
fearful for our safety.

We search to feel within the rhythm that is unfolding life.
We listen to hear the voice of Silence guiding us to trust our body wisdom.
We awaken to the pulsations and contractions and expansions of our soulbody.

Ignorance falls like holy sweat,
the birthing waters of a Christ heart,
a human heart,
wonderfully alive!

Bibliography

Adyashanti. *Resurrecting Jesus: Embodying the Spirit of a Revolutionary Mystic.* Boulder, CO: Sounds True, 2016.
Almaas, A. H. *Elements of the Real in Man.* Diamond Heart 1. Boston: Shambhala, 2000.
———. *Facets of Unity: The Enneagram of Holy Ideas.* Berkeley: Diamond, 1998.
———. *Luminous Night's Journey.* Berkeley: Diamond, 1996.
———. *The Point of Existence: Transformations of Narcissism in Self-Realization.* Diamond Mind 3. Boston: Shambhala, 2001.
Almaas, A. H., and Karen Johnson. *The Power of Divine Eros: The Illuminating Force of Love in Everyday Life.* Boston: Shambhala, 2013.
Anglican Church in Aotearoa, New Zealand and Polynesia. *A New Zealand Prayer Book.* Auckland, NZ: Anglican Church in Aotearoa, New Zealand and Polynesia, 1988. https://anglicanprayerbook.nz/.
Armstrong, Karen. *The Great Transformation: The Beginning of Our Religious Traditions.* New York: Knopf, 2006.
Augustine. *The Confessions.* Translated by Maria Boulding. New York: New City, 1997.
Barnstone, Willis, and Marvin Meyer, eds. *The Gnostic Bible: Gnostic Texts of Mystical Wisdom from the Ancient and Medieval Worlds.* Boston: Shambhala, 2003.
Beck, Don Edward, and Christopher C. Cowan. *Spiral Dynamics: Mastering Values, Leadership, and Change.* Malden: Blackwell, 1996.
Bellah, Robert N. *Religion in Human Evolution: From the Paleolithic to the Axial Age.* Cambridge: Belknap, 2011.
Berry, Wendell. *Sabbaths.* San Francisco: North Point, 1987.
Block, Melissa. "Theodore Parker and the 'Moral Universe.'" NPR, Sept. 2, 2010. https://www.npr.org/2010/09/02/129609461/theodore-parker-and-the-moral-universe.
Borg, Marcus J., and John Dominic Crossan. *The First Christmas: What the Gospels Really Teach About Jesus's Birth.* New York: HarperOne, 2009.
Bourgeault, Cynthia. *The Wisdom Jesus: Transforming Heart and Mind—A New Perspective on Christ and His Message.* Boulder: Shambhala, 2008.
Brock, Rita Nakashima, and Rebecca Ann Parker. *Proverbs of Ashes: Violence, Redemptive Suffering, and the Search for What Saves Us.* Boston: Beacon, 2001.
Bruteau, Beatrice. *Radical Optimism: Practical Spirituality in an Uncertain World.* Boulder: Sentient, 2002.

Bibliography

Buber, Martin. *I and Thou*. New York: Scribner, 1957.
Butcher, Carmen Acevedo, trans. *The Cloud of Unknowing*. Boston: Shambhala, 2009.
Byrne, Mary E., trans. "Be Thou My Vision." Versified by Eleanor H. Hull. Hymnary, 1927. https://hymnary.org/text/be_thou_my_vision_o_lord_of_my_heart.
Chestnut, Beatrice. *The Complete Enneagram: 27 Paths to Greater Self-Knowledge*. Berkeley: She Writes, 2013.
Chilton, Bruce. *Rabbi Jesus: An Intimate Biography*. New York: PRH Christian, 2002.
Chödrön, Pema. *When Things Fall Apart: Heart Advice for Difficult Times*. 20th anniv. ed. Boulder: Shambhala, 2016.
Dana, Deb. *The Polyvagal Theory in Therapy: Engaging the Rhythm of Regulation*. New York: Norton, 2018.
De Mello, Anthony. *Awakening: Conversations with the Master*. Chicago: Loyola, 1998.
Douglas-Klotz, Neil. *Revelations of the Aramaic Jesus: The Hidden Teachings on Life and Death*. Newburyport, MA: Hampton Roads, 2022.
Eckhart, Meister. "Sermon Fifteen: How A Radical Letting Go Becomes a True Letting Be." In *Passion for Creation: The Earth-Honoring Spirituality of Meister Eckhart*, edited by Matthew Fox, 213–17. Rochester, VT: Inner Traditions, 2000.
———. "Sermon Nine: Waking Up to the Nearness of God's Kingdom." In *Passion for Creation: The Earth-Honoring Spirituality of Meister Eckhart*, edited by Matthew Fox, 137–40. Rochester, VT: Inner Traditions, 2000.
———. "Sermon Twelve: Sinking Eternally into God." In *Passion for Creation: The Earth-Honoring Spirituality of Meister Eckhart*, edited by Matthew Fox, 177–80. Rochester, VT: Inner Traditions, 2000.
Faber, Frederick William. "There's a Wideness in God's Mercy." Hymnary, 1862. https://hymnary.org/text/theres_a_wideness_in_gods_mercy.
Gebser, Jean. *The Ever-Present Origin*. Translated by Noel Barstad with Algis Mickunas. Athens, Ohio University Press, 1985.
Greenberg, Jay R., and Stephen A. Mitchell. *Object Relations in Psychoanalytic Theory*. Cambridge: Harvard University Press, 1983.
Gurdjieff, G. I. *Beelzebub's Tales to His Grandson*. New York: Penguin, 1999.
———. *Life Is Real Only Then, When "I Am."* New York: Penguin, 1978.
Harari, Yuval Noah. *Sapiens: A Brief History of Humankind*. New York: Harper, 2015.
Helminski, Kabir. *The Knowing Heart: A Sufi Path of Transformation*. Boston: Shambhala, 2000.
Helminski, Kabir, and Ahmad Rezwani, trans. *Love's Ripening: Rumi on the Heart's Journey*. Boston: Shambhala, 2010.
Hilmi, Ahmet. *Awakened Dreams: Raji's Journeys with the Mirror Dede*. Translated by Refik Algan and Camille Helminski. Boston: Shambhala, 1993.
John of the Cross. "The Dark Night of the Soul." Translated by David Lewis. London: Baker, 1908. https://www.poetryfoundation.org/poems/157984/the-dark-night-of-the-soul.
Julian of Norwich. *Showings*. Translated by Edmund Colledge and James Walsh. Classics of Western Spirituality. New York: Paulist, 1978.
Kalanithi, Paul. *When Breath Becomes Air*. New York: Random House, 2016.
Kornfield, Jack. *A Path with Heart: A Guide Through the Perils and Promises of Spiritual Life*. New York: Scribner, 1993.
Krishnamurti, J. *Freedom from the Known*. Edited by Mary Lutyens. New York: HarperOne, 1969.

Bibliography

Levine, Peter A. *In an Unspoken Voice: How the Body Releases Trauma and Restores Goodness.* Berkeley: North Atlantic, 2010.

Maitri, Sandra. *The Spiritual Dimension of the Enneagram: Nine Faces of the Soul.* New York: Tarcher, 2000.

Maté, Gabor. *In the Realm of Hungry Ghosts: Close Encounters with Addiction.* Berkeley: North Atlantic, 2010.

McGinn, Bernard, ed. *Meister Eckhart and the Beguine Mystics: Hadewijch of Brabant, Mechthild of Magdeburg, and Marguerite Porete.* New York: Continuum, 1997.

———. *The Mystical Thought of Meister Eckhart: The Man from Whom God Hid Nothing.* New York: Crossroad, 2001.

Merrill, Nan C. *Psalms for Praying: An Invitation to Wholeness.* New York: Continuum, 2002.

O'Donohue, John. *To Bless the Space Between Us: A Book of Blessings.* New York: Convergent, 2008.

O'Neal, David, ed. *Meister Eckhart from Whom God Hid Nothing: Sermons, Writings, and Sayings.* Boston: Shambhala, 1996.

Pagels, Elaine. *Beyond Belief: The Secret Gospel of Thomas.* New York: Vintage, 2004.

Palmer, G. H. E., et al., trans. *Philokalia: The Eastern Christian Spiritual Texts.* Annotated by Allyne Smith. Skylight Illuminations. Woodstock, VT: Skylight Paths, 2006.

Palmer, Martin. *The Jesus Sutras: Rediscovering the Lost Scrolls of Taoist Christianity.* New York: Ballantine, 2001.

Porete, Marguerite. *The Mirror of Simple Souls.* Translated by Ellen L. Babinsky. Classics of Western Spirituality. New York: Paulist, 1993.

Rahner, Karl. *Foundations of Christian Faith: An Introduction to the Idea of Christianity.* Translated by William V. Dych. New York: Seabury, 1978.

Ricoeur, Paul. *From Text to Action: Essays in Hermeneutics, II.* Translated by Kathleen Blamey and John B. Thompson. Northwestern University Studies in Phenomenology and Existential Philosophy. Evanston: Northwestern University Press, 1991.

———. *Hermeneutics and the Human Sciences: Essays on Language, Action and Interpretation.* Edited and translated by John B. Thompson. Cambridge: Cambridge University Press, 1981.

Riegert, Ray, and Thomas Moore, eds. *The Lost Sutras of Jesus: Unlocking the Ancient Wisdom of the Xian Monks.* Translated by Jon Babcock. Berkeley: Ulysses, 2003.

Riso, Don Richard, and Russ Hudson. *The Wisdom of the Enneagram: The Complete Guide to Psychological and Spiritual Growth for the Nine Personality Types.* New York: Bantam, 1999.

Roberts, Bernadette. *The Path to No-Self.* Albany: State University of New York Press, 1991.

Rumi, Mevlana Jelaluddin. *The Essential Rumi.* Translated by Coleman Barks with John Moyne. New York: HarperSanFrancisco, 1995.

———. "Out beyond ideas of wrongdoing and right doing." In *Rumi: The Book of Love; Poems of Ecstasy and Longing,* translated by Coleman Barks et al., 123. New York: HarperCollins, 2003.

———. "There Is Some Kiss We Want." Translated by Coleman Barks. Poetry Chaikhana. https://www.poetry-chaikhana.com/Poets/R/RumiMevlanaJ/Thereissomek/index.html.

Stefon, Matt. "The Axial Age: 5 Fast Facts." *Encyclopedia Britannica*, Sept. 21, 2015. https://www.britannica.com/list/the-axial-age-5-fast-facts.

Bibliography

Stern, Daniel N. *The Interpersonal World of The Infant: A View from Psychoanalysis and Developmental Psychology*. New York: Basic, 2000.

———. *The Present Moment in Psychotherapy and Everyday Life*. New York: Norton, 2004.

Taussig, Hal, ed. *A New New Testament: A Bible for the Twenty-First Century, Combining Traditional and Newly Discovered Texts*. Boston: Mariner, 2013.

Taylor, Charles. *Sources of the Self: The Making of the Modern Identity*. Cambridge: Harvard University Press, 1989.

Thew Forrester, Kevin G. *Holding Beauty in My Soul's Arms: A Guide for Post-Modern Pilgrims Seeking Authentic Spiritual Transformation*. Leeds, MA: LeaderResources, 2011.

Weil, Simone. *Gravity and Grace*. Translated by Arthur Wills. Lincoln: University of Nebraska Press, 1997.

Wilber, Ken. *Integral Psychology: Consciousness, Spirit, Psychology, Therapy*. Boston: Shambhala, 2000.

———. *Integral Spirituality: A Startling New Role for Religion in the Modern and Postmodern World*. Boston: Integral, 2006.

———. *Sex, Ecology, Spirituality: The Spirit of Evolution*. Boston: Shambhala, 2000.

KEVIN G. THEW FORRESTER, Episcopal priest, is a teacher of mediation, body practice, and the Enneagram. He received Jukai from Shoken Winecoff, is an authorized instructor of Diamond Body Practice, and a certified teacher of the Enneagram in the Narrative tradition. He is the author of *Beyond My Wants, Beyond My Fears* (2016), *Holding Beauty in My Soul's Arms* (2011), and *I Have Called You Friends* (2003). He is a contributing essayist for Progressing Spirit.

www.ingramcontent.com/pod-product-compliance
Lightning Source LLC
Chambersburg PA
CBHW051634230426
43669CB00013B/2304